# DEDICATION

Dedicated to my dear wife Barbara who for fifty-eight years
showed me the true quality and value of life.

# CONTENTS

# WINGS ACROSS THE GREAT DIVIDE

**The sequel to**
*The Flight of the Mew Gull*
**and**
*Sigh for a Merlin*

**by**

## ALEX HENSHAW

**CIRRUS ASSOCIATES**

PUBLISHED BY:
Cirrus Associates (S.W.)
Kington Magna
GILLINGHAM
Dorset
SP8 5EW UK

**ISBN 1 902807 19 7**

PRINTED IN ENGLAND BY:
Bath Press Ltd.
Lower Bristol Road
BATH
BA2 3BL

PHOTO SCANNING BY:
International Graphics Services Ltd.
24-31 Fourth Avenue
Westfield Trading Estate
Radstock
BATH
BA3 4XE

Maps based on material © 1994 Magellan Geographix
Map design by James Campbell

DISTRIBUTORS:
Cirrus Associates (S.W.)
Kington Magna
GILLINGHAM
Dorset
SP8 5EW UK

COVER: Michael Turner's painting depicts a hair-raising night take-off in a Miles Gemini by the author from Agadir in 1948.

# ACKNOWLEDGEMENTS

Preparing this book for publication on behalf of Alex Henshaw, a personal friend for many years, has been a privilege and I wish to record my gratitude to him for entrusting me with the editing and production of this third and final part of his autobiography.

A number of friends have helped out by providing additional information and supplying photographs for this book. To Michael Oakey (Editor of *Aeroplane*), Julian Temple, Ron Moulton, Philip Jarrett, Roger T. Jackson and the Museum of Berkshire Aviation I convey my sincere thanks.

I would also like to thank publisher Peter Campbell for his support and encouragement throughout the production of this book.

**Richard Riding**

# PREFACE

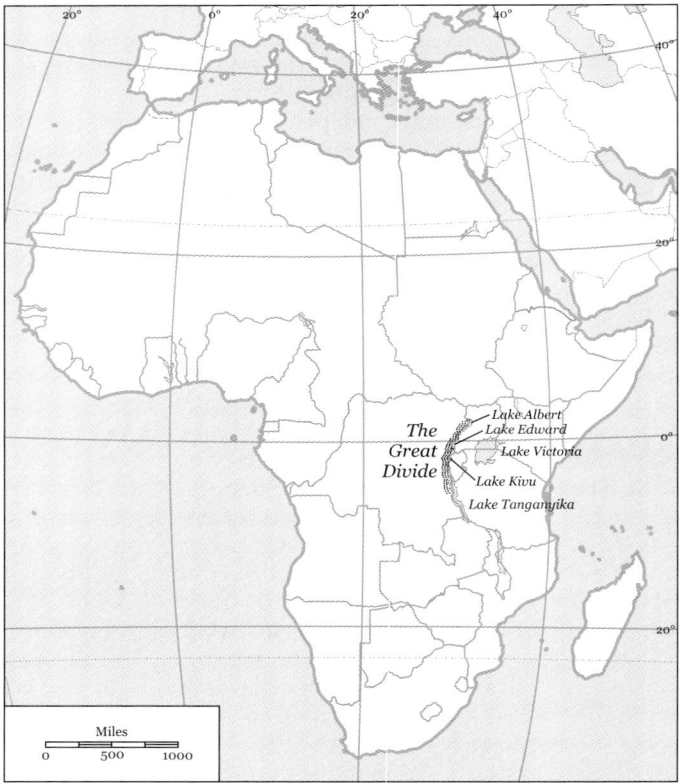

"When we flew low over Bukavu and followed a steep narrow cleft that disgorged enormous volumes of water from Lake Kivu into its large sister Lake Tanganyika, another facet of this intriguing continent gave me food for thought. I had been to many countries where geographical interest is taken in the Great Divide, where a ridge of very high ground causes the water, accumulating as rain, to run one way or another. The area over which we were now flying gave clear indication that, not only did this vast volume of water flow over the Equator to the Mediterranean thousands of miles away through the historic Nile, but from the same source flowed the mighty Zambesi on its way to the Indian Ocean, and also its even mightier twin, the Congo, winding almost unseen to the Atlantic. The knowledge that these three giant rivers flowed north, east and west from this spot absorbed me in deep thought and I could think of no other country that featured a phenomenon of such magnitude."

# FOREWORD

by Ian Hay

Whilst Alex Henshaw was writing his new book he telephoned me to ask if I would do him the honour of writing his foreword. To have this request from a good and true friend, the honour, on the contrary, was purely mine.

I first came across Alex some years before the Second World War when, as a very young man, he became noteworthy in the King's Cup and other air races in Britain. Alex subsequently moved on in 1939 to establish air records in the single-seat Mew Gull to and from the Cape. Some 62 years later these records remain unsurpassed. His modest accounts of these incredible flights are recorded in his book *The Flight of the Mew Gull*. Alex went on to distinguish himself in the world of aviation as a test pilot for Vickers-Armstrongs, testing some hundreds of Spitfires and Lancaster bombers during the war years. For his general performance throughout he received, I believe, meagre recognition.

On the conclusion of the war in Europe in 1945, the General Mining & Finance Corporation in South Africa formed, as a subsidiary company under the chairmanship of my uncle Sir George Albu, Miles Aircraft of South Africa (Pty) to pave the way for sales of civilian aircraft when they became available. When I, like so many, was seeking employment after the war, I became a member of this company through having worked for Miles Aircraft at Woodley airfield near Reading at the end of the war. Early in 1946 we were joined in South Africa by Alex when he flew the first Miles Messenger out to Johannesburg, followed some four months later by his wife Barbara and small son Alex Jnr. After his survey flight and subsequent record flights in the 1930s, Alex was no stranger to the sub-continent, and to South Africa in particular.

With much hard work we did manage to sell a few aircraft in the Belgian Congo (as it then was), Kenya, Portugese East Africa (now Mozambique), and generally in the Union of South Africa. When the Miles Gemini, a twin-engined version of the Messenger, was delivered to us here in South Africa it was sold without delay. But further sales of the Gemini proved extremely difficult as they, like the Messenger, were of all-wood construction and were considered unsuitable in the prevailing climatic conditions.

Alex and I encountered many hilarious experiences, either together or as individuals, during the course of our operations. But for Alex's great sense of humour the company might well have shut up shop earlier than it did. However, we kept going until the liquidation of Miles in England that led in turn to the liquidation of Miles Aircraft in South Africa. Alex then returned to the UK to follow his interests there.

Thereafter we kept in close contact through the years and I am happy to say that this association is still maintained more than 50 years later. Our interest in aviation has never waned and it still gives us great joy to talk about former colleagues and service personnel, though most have sadly gone.

I look forward to reading this latest publication which, I believe, will reveal some of the happy times we spent together in Africa. The mere fact that he has written this book at this stage of his life reveals the determination and spirit of a great man. May you receive joy from it, as I know I shall.

**Ian Hay**
Everton, Natal, South Africa
September 24th, 2001

# AUTHOR'S NOTE

Any degree of success that *Flight Of The Mew Gull* and *Sigh For A Merlin* may have had is due in great part to my late wife, Barbara. Numerous friends anticipated that *Wings Across The Great Divide* would follow to complete the saga of my years in the air. However, when Barbara died in November 1996, life, as I had known it for 58 years, ended. In addition to losing interest in completing my autobiographical trilogy there was the fact that there are incidents in this final part of my story of which I am not proud: in fact, in certain instances I am ashamed. In particular I recall an exploratory Gemini flight with my wife and young son (see Chapter 8), when we crossed the endless expanse of steaming Congo jungle and got embroiled in violent electrical storms. The stupidity of a venture that so nearly ended our lives churns my stomach and sickens me to this day.

Similarly, the enforced landing during a wild and black winter's night on the unlit marshland at Maldon in Essex (see Chapter 7), when fate alone guided me to the only level patch of arable on which to land undamaged. Then, on the following morning, only the Almighty could have created a gale-force wind in the right direction in which to take off. Without this divine intervention the machine would have suffered the ignominious indignity of being dismantled and loaded on to a lorry.

For both these transgressions I would have rated the airmanship as unworthy for a man of my experience; more the actions of a young adventurous novice who would learn the hard way that it is wiser to give greater consideration to weather forecasts.

I do not regret the incident at Agadir (see Chapter 10), considering that the war had barely ended. I gained some satisfaction in treating the French occupants with the contempt they deserved, but at the same time I do now appreciate, more than I did at the time, that in shooting at the Gemini they could also have killed my old friend Colonel Jacques Lorentz.

To hand this kind of material over to another writer would, in my opinion, leave it open to embellishment and distortion of the facts, which would be an injustice to my family and those friends who know me well. Indeed, over recent years, several well-known writers have approached me with a view to publishing a biography. My refusal was based not so much on immodesty but rather the fact that truth is often stranger than fiction, and should be told accurately and without embellishment. In 1998 Richard Riding, founder of *Aeroplane Monthly* and editor for 25 years, took early retirement. Richard and I have been friends for a long time and I had come to respect his work, professionalism and integrity. As he has been a frequent visitor to our home for more than 20 years, there is no doubt that he had come to know Barbara and myself better than most. As my 90th year commenced, the question of an illustrated biography covering my entire life was discussed and, at the same time, the feasibility of completing the final part of my trilogy upon which I had been so consciously assisted by my late wife. Richard not only volunteered to edit and produce *Wings Across The Great Divide* but also agreed to research material and photographs covering my life for an illustrated biography to be published after my death. To these ends Richard has been given a free hand and unlimited access to a prodigious amount of material in the form of personal letters, numerous endorsed books, hundreds of photographs and a mass of memorabilia. In order to ensure accuracy my son Alex will assist Richard with more personal matters, but in order not to inhibit any appraisal that Richard may care to make, the contents will not be perused or questioned by me at any time.

I have never found writing about myself easy. The fact that my earlier books have never been out of print in over a quarter of a century is possibly an acknowledgement that the period in which I was involved has historical importance and interest, rather than any contribution I may have made to it.

My old friend Jeffrey Quill and I had, in many ways, parallel flying lives; when discussing the subject of autobiographies we both reached the conclusion that it was better for those who had been involved to describe events and incidents first-hand, rather than entrust the task to an imaginative writer with an eye to glamourise and embellish the facts to boost book sales.

I have put my trust in Richard, both as a friend and working associate, confident in the knowledge that my family will not be disappointed with his work.

# CHAPTER 1

# REFLECTIONS

"If only I could have my life over again." Whenever I hear that poignantly sad utterance for some reason I feel embarrassed, as if my own good fortune through life has, in some strange way, precluded others from their own fair share. I think I can honestly say that on reflecting upon my own past I have only two regrets.

I would like to have competed in the World Aerobatic Championships. At the time these were deferred because of the war and in any case I did not then have the means to acquire the specialist type of machine required, or meet the heavy costs involved.

My second regret is that, despite flying military aircraft for the duration of the war, I never fired a shot in anger. This may seem somewhat surprising bearing in mind that during the war I had been allocated two armed Spitfires for personal use in protecting the Vickers-Armstrongs Castle Bromwich works at which I was then chief test pilot. In the first instance there had been a great deal of head-scratching when RAF Fighter Command became aware that I was a civilian who had never served in the forces. I had completed gunnery and combat exercises with various fighter squadrons but the fact remained that, in the unlikely event of my falling into enemy hands, I could be shot as a *franc-tireur*.

I never at any time had any pre-conceived romantic notions as to my likely success, or otherwise, as a fighter pilot. It was, however, impossible during those prewar years, with Hitler and the rapidly-expanding Nazi air force boasting of their prowess as they tramped across peaceful and unprotected countries, not to be more than aware that one day I should do what our fathers had done some 20 years before.

I was not keen on the idea of flying a heavy bomber, but with my considerable experience of high-performance racing aircraft I expected that I would go automatically into a fighter squadron at the outbreak of war and that the outcome would be fast, furious and final. In spite of the fact that I was within a whisker of being commissioned on three occasions, fate ordained that I should not go into the Royal Air Force.

As I look back, there were long spells when I hated my job at Castle Bromwich. Ever since I became aware of Hitler, when my father and I flew to several enjoyable Teutonic functions, all flamboyantly organised with a military slant, I became convinced that our countries would one day clash. Throughout those golden years of flying we all hoped fervently that war with Germany would never materialise. Notwithstanding any apparent complacency, I prepared myself mentally for the heartache and horror that war would bring.

Having said that, I would be the first to acknowledge that the constant demands made upon me at Castle Bromwich did in many ways stimulate my own efforts to succeed. Not only was there a meticulous level of flying in critical conditions, there was also the responsibility of endeavouring to maintain efficiency, output and morale with all those who worked on an airfield often suffering from the appalling effects of air raids.

In this regard I was greatly helped by the fact that the airfield and flight-shed personnel were divorced from the main offices and factory. This meant that I could 'run' the show on a very tight rein, which in turn meant that I had to set the example both in the air and on the ground. I should certainly never have had this measure of control and success without a compliant managing director, who not only understood what I was endeavouring to achieve but with whom there was mutual trust. I do not think it was easy for either of us at first to come to terms.

When I joined Vickers-Armstrongs I was almost 27 years old and the only boss I had ever had was my father. Throughout those formative working years within our extensive and complex family business, he would delegate matters to me with the persuasive comforting words: "You can sort that little problem out, son," and then leave me to get on with it.

I adored my father and all I wanted to do was make him proud of what I could achieve; thus everything that I tackled became close and personal. I made many mistakes that would make me feel like a thrashed dog, but I never forgot, particularly when Dad silently reviewed my work and, full of enthusiasm, went over each problem in detail. Then, after a moment's reflection, he would say: "Never mind, son – you'll know next time."

At the outbreak of war in September 1939 I went to Vickers at Weybridge, where my boss was the aggressive and forceful Trevor Westbrook, who had a reputation for getting things done. On being shown into Westbrook's office by chief test pilot 'Mutt' Summers I was given a tough briefing. In fact it was a vigorous 'pep' talk I felt was quite unnecessary. But it suited my own attitude and all went well. However, when I resigned, after a short and most unsatisfactory spell, and told him in pretty blunt terms that I was leaving, he nearly exploded.

After the fateful and fortuitous meeting with Jeffrey Quill my next boss at Supermarine was Mr Pratt, a very nice, kind family type of man. After Jeffrey had 'done the rounds' and introduced me to all the senior staff with whom I would be working, I felt I was about to join one large happy and enthusiastic family. Sadly, Mr Pratt took his own life shortly afterwards; no doubt the pressures and vicissitudes of war had taken their toll.

The main Supermarine offices and mess looked out over the Solent and the River Itchen. At that period of the war we were really conscious of being at the heart of things. From the slipway we would tow or guide our flying boats past silent yet menacing ships of war for testing in quieter waters.

Following Pratt's sad death he was replaced by Commander Sir James

Bird, who had formerly been closely associated with the company. I liked Jimmy Bird immediately but, as I was appointed chief test pilot at Castle Bromwich soon after his arrival, I only met him socially when he visited the Directors' resident home in Four Oaks for informal discussions. Tragically, he also committed suicide soon afterwards.

As already outlined in *Sigh for a Merlin*, there were many times when I regretted my job at Castle Bromwich. But in the final analysis I accept that it was a challenge that suited my own character and temperament and enabled me to give of my best.

On June 15, 1940 I motored with my wife Barbara through the night to fly my first Castle Bromwich Spitfire. On my arrival I was met by Sir Alex Dunbar, formerly of Vickers-Armstrongs at Weybridge. Apparently he had been hoisted out of bed at four in the morning, only to be told by the irrepressible Lord Beaverbrook to get off his backside and join the perspiring group of managers, inspectors, AID men and women and all the other willing helpers frantically trying to complete this Castle Bromwich Spitfire for flight trials. Athough I liked Dunbar I found him somewhat aloof, conscious of his position and lacking any knowledge of the practical side of flying. Like so many during that critical period Dunbar, though gifted with commercial acumen, found it difficult to come to terms with his speedy elevation.

It was during Dunbar's management that a furore arose over a Spitfire display I gave that brought the city of Birmingham to a standstill. I was always deferential and carried out my instructions to the letter. When Dunbar telephoned and asked me to display over Birmingham's civic centre he brushed aside my attempt at a mild protestation, saying he had discussed the whole matter with the Lord Mayor and he wished the display to be executed in my usual style over the Council Chambers. The repercussions of this display were almost catastrophic and when the Chief Constable and his cavalcade of police cars came to apprehend me I had some satisfaction in suggesting he should first have a word with the managing director and his Lord Mayor! My display had brought all traffic to a standstill and I know that I could have made it a little milder. But I remember starting my first dive from 5,000 ft over the vast city with its sea of shops, schools and factories and mile upon mile of suburbia. This sprawl extended in every direction and, had I had a failure of any sort, not only would I have lost my own life, it could have cost the lives of many innocent onlookers. I was so angry at the stupidity of such an egotistical gesture by Dunbar and the Lord Mayor I decided that someone should be taught a lesson.

During that early period of the war it became obvious to those like myself that something was not quite right about the factory, despite all the expertise from Supermarine and Vickers-Armstrongs. Bombing day and night, with the 'blood' trains of Dunkirk unloading for the Midlands hospitals during the dead of night, did nothing to boost morale or allay fears that at any moment we could, as Churchill had recently announced in Parliament, be fighting on the beaches, in the hills, in the towns and on the streets.

My own work at this time was both frustrating and difficult. The production of aircraft was spasmodic and thus accentuated the problems of flight-testing. There would be days when the weather was good but no aircraft were ready for test. Then, as Saturday approached, a cavalcade of aircraft would be seen crawling across the road on the way to the airfield. More often than not the ever-changing weather made my work tedious and demanding, and requiring unnecessary risk. To my way of thinking there was little doubt that something was wrong in our operation or management of the works. Now faced with the responsibility for keeping the ever-increasing numbers of men and women employed at the flight-sheds, I found it very difficult to keep them on their toes and pulling their weight.

Sir Alex Dunbar was soon replaced and Major Hew Kilner took the post of managing director. His appointment did not appear to improve morale, nor did it help with my own situation. Kilner was a nice person but I found that we got on much better outside the confines of Vickers-Armstrongs, when we met and dined in our respective homes. Thankfully I was only involved in only one small *contretemps* with Kilner before he was transferred to another Vickers works.

One day I had landed with a list of snags and was engrossed with ground staff when I noticed a tall elderly gentleman, clad in a light overcoat and wearing a trilby hat, watching the proceedings from a short distance away. The moment I had finished he came towards me with outstretched hand and said: "Alex, Dickson's my name – I have just taken over Kilner's office." He looked me straight in the eye and asked if we could go through the three huge Castle Bromwich flight-sheds and discuss any problems with which I was faced. I liked him immediately.

Dickson was the first and only Castle Bromwich managing director who had devoted time and effort to visit me at the flight-sheds purely for the opportunity to help me with my own work. Though he had little or no experience with aircraft, having just come from a small engineering plant at Dartford, it quickly became apparent that Dick not only understood works management but knew how to handle men and women. Right from the start there was mutual trust and, although there were anxious moments, slowly but surely Castle Bromwich began to demonstrate its true potential, to the point of ultimately becoming the showcase of British industry at war. Barbara and I became life-long friends of Dick and his wife Dorrie and our parting, after nearly five stressful and anxious years under extreme pressure, was akin to a son and daughter bidding farewell to parents. All the directors at Castle Bromwich and subsequently other Vickers shops or armament factories were awarded knighthoods – Dick received the C.B.E.

There is little doubt that the unusual manner in which the top echelons of the Vickers-Armstrongs management and myself had to mix caused a degree of uncertainty, if not embarrassment. In those few halcyon weeks before the outbreak of war I had become a very high profile figure, having broken all records flying from London to Cape Town and back – records, incidentally, that remain unbroken at the time of writing. I would be a hypocrite if I were to say that I did not relish the new-found success that opened all doors to me. At heart I am a very simple person and enjoy the countryside and open way of life. To receive mountains of fan mail, invitations by the score and be unable to walk down a street in town or dine in a London restaurant without being addressed, no matter how effusively or plausibly, can be somewhat unnerving. My life was not my own, particularly when telephone switchboard girls made excuses to ring, or reporters and journalists surreptitiously took early morning snapshots as Dad and I exercised our horses on the lovely golden beach near our Lincolnshire home.

When Neville Chamberlain made his historic announcement that Britain and Germany were at war this state of affairs ended in a flash. I breathed a sigh of relief, able once more to move around with impunity without anyone taking the slightest notice. Whilst the press continued to publish small items, such as my appointment with Supermarine, it was almost as though I had never existed, a situation that prevailed right up to my marriage in February 1940. Barbara's feeling about publicity was the same as my own and the last thing she wanted was a spectacular socialite wedding. I had little time to deal with the final arrangements but when a national newspaper announced: *"Famous airman to marry Countess de Chateaubrun in Cathedral Wedding,"* Barbara took matters into her own hands and had the wedding banns published with a date three weeks ahead. In the meantime she had obtained a special licence that enabled us to meet at Westminster Cathedral with our immediate family to discreetly and quietly make our solemn vows. Afterwards we went for a delightful lunch and then drove through deep snow to Supermarine so that I could continue with my job the following morning.

I was able to enjoy my anonymity for quite a time, until the first important demonstration of a Spitfire Mk II was arranged for Service chiefs of the Allied powers. To my astonishment, when the members of the press escorting the VIP party on to the tarmac stepped out of their cars I was regaled with calls from many of the pressmen whom I had known during the halcyon days of peace. I gave the best display that I could, and after an embarrassing session of answering a barrage of questions the meeting broke up and the whole circus departed. The next morning I was shown headlines in the *Daily Telegraph* that read " . . . did everything in a remarkable display but set it on fire." As a newcomer to the Spitfire, and having such good friends as Jeffrey Quill and George Pickering, I was irritated and annoyed. It was also of dubious consolation to the organisers of the mission, or our own staff members, as the meeting was strictly classified and places and names had to be used with discretion.

Although my training had been with working men and women, with whom I generally worked well, this was the first time in my life that I was made aware of the potential minefield encountered when dealing with the different elements within industry, with all their own departmental rules and regulations. The Aeronautical Inspection Directorate (AID) was the first to become my *bête noire*. True, I had dealt with inspectors of that very worthy organisation ever since I owned my first aeroplane. My involvement with the AID became much closer while preparing the Mew Gull for racing and record-breaking flights, as both engine and airframe required extensive and unusual modification. AID had to approve each and every one of these alterations, some requiring qualified professional approval in an aeronautical laboratory. The inspectors were competent and experienced engineers who knew their jobs, and as a pilot I was thankful for them on more than one occasion. My position at Castle Bromwich was complex in a number of ways. Whilst I was employed by Vickers-Armstrongs as the company's chief test pilot, Vickers-Armstrongs managed the factory but it was owned by the Ministry of Aircraft Production (M.A.P.). The aircraft produced were the property of M.A.P. and the offices of the AID branch were located in the same block as our senior staff. After aircraft were towed on to the airfield for flight they were first inspected by our own inspection department before being handed over to AID for further scrutiny. I never really thought much about this system until I found myself under extreme pressure, flight testing under adverse conditions and responsible for all that took place on the airfield. The demand in all branches of the industry meant that the calibre of the workforce was not always up to the standard with which we had become accustomed. The authority of the AID officers was sacrosanct and no machine could leave the ground until the 1090 certificate had been signed by one of the senior and approved inspectors. Some of the newly-appointed inspectors were young and inexperienced but, worst of all, they were sometimes conscious of their authority and abused it. An AID inspector would conduct the engine ground-run before flight. I was often very irritated to see one of my pilots standing out on the tarmac in a cold wind whilst an inspector, after spending useless minutes going over every point in the cockpit, then procrastinated over the starting procedure with a studied concentration on warming up the engine almost up to its maximum temperature. All this I invariably bore in silence, until one day, as I was kept waiting alongside the machine during a ground run, the AID inspector throttled back the engine and from the cockpit said: "It's u/s, down on the revs." I immediately jumped up on to the port wing, pushed home the de Havilland two-pitch propeller control into fine pitch and said to the inspector: "I think you'll find the revs OK now."

Another area which I found difficulty in handling was overtime. My own attitude was that we worked round the clock if the situation so demanded. I think my own longest stint at that time was the occasion when I left the house at 2.45 am and finally flopped into bed as the clock struck midnight. The AID, being a Civil Service department, was governed by rigid rules which covered holidays, daily hours, days in the week or even the total time occupied at work during a month. Heads of departments had great difficulty in co-operating with someone like myself, no matter how willing I was to comply.

I resigned myself to accepting this situation until one cold and wet November day, when the weather was marginal and not a single machine was available for flight. Later that afternoon a whole line of Spitfires could be seen being towed by tractors across the Chester road. During the customary long wait while the aircraft were given a final inspection I noticed that my own firm's chief inspector was having what appeared to be an acrimonious discussion with the head of AID. On walking over I was told by the inspector that he would not sign the flight certificate until the next morning, because in his opinion the weather was now too bad for flying. The details of this incident have already been recounted in *Sigh for a Merlin*; suffice to say that the outcome was such that I never experienced any further problems with AID! Although it was difficult at times we worked together harmoniously and efficiently, as any well-balanced and well-managed organisation should.

Another aspect of my job at that time was the large number of official missions and visits. Service Chiefs of Staff, political heads of Allied and neutral countries, as well as the various leaders of our Parliamentary groups, all wished to keep themselves in the limelight by paying lip service to what had become the one fighter production factory they wished to see. On being briefed on each visit by Dick I made sure that the flying, be it a demonstration of a Lancaster, formation flying or my own display was meticulously scheduled to the last degree. We must have had hundreds of these sessions during the war but at the time, to my mind at least, their relationship to the more serious and productive work in hand was so insignificant I did not even record such events in my log-book. Most of the demonstrations were purely a publicity exercise and the expertise in putting an aircraft through its paces was elementary and could have been executed by any competent display pilot. The calibre and status of the visitors, however, varied enormously. King George VI made visits but I found King Haakon of Norway the most outgoing and friendly of the royal monarchs. Political heads from almost every country with whom we were not at war came to Castle Bromwich, as well as Mrs Eleanor Roosevelt.

There was however one visit that stood head and shoulders above all others. Special Branch had briefed me with the news that Prime Minister Winston Churchill wished to see a demonstration of our latest Spitfire. I had admired and respected Churchill since my childhood, when my father told me of the exploits of this adventurous and courageous young man, and of the shameful treatment he received with the failure of the Dardanelles campaign. In my book Winston Churchill is the greatest Englishman of all time and the saviour of the free world when other leaders would have capitulated our nation which, in all probability, would have imperilled the entire world.

After performing my solo display I was usually introduced to members of any visiting deputation and then, in the case of aviation representatives, would adjourn to my office to discuss more serious technicalities. On this occasion Lord Dudley ushered me to the VIP group with the Duke and Duchess of Marlborough, when Commander Thompson, making his apologies, guided me over to Mr and Mrs Churchill, who had asked for chairs to be brought out. I felt a little embarrassed when Commander Thompson beckoned me to sit in the chair next to Mr Churchill, to the exclusion of others nearby. The discussion must have carried on for some time. I learnt later from Lord Dudley that Churchill had been so engrossed in conversation during his visit that his entourage and the special train had been kept 20 minutes longer than their tight schedule had allowed for.

Other VIP visits were less enjoyable, particularly when Dick would whisper in my ear as I prepared for a demonstration: "They come not to praise but to bury."

During the early part of the war the Spitfire did not have the aura of fame that it later achieved. There were those who had become sceptical of its performance and wished to see the machine in flight for themselves. The critical observers turned out to be missions from the USA, Turkey, Sweden, France and Russia. In such instances my display was one of precision and concentration, for it was my job to demonstrate the Spitfire's precise manoeuvrability and superior performance over other fighter aircraft.

I look back on those grim years at Castle Bromwich with a degree of sombre satisfaction. So many who must have hated my guts for the pressures to which they were subjected subsequently became life-long dear friends.

# CHAPTER 2

# TO FLY OR NOT TO FLY

The fresh breeze with the tang of salt and seaweed blew into my face and I was brought abruptly back to earth. I was so deep in thought as we ambled up the rough off-road pull-over that I was quite unconscious of the fact that we had reached the top. Even my very young son Alex, jigging excitedly alongside in his eagerness to paddle, had not roused me from my thoughts.

On the brow of the pull-over we gazed at an expanse of clean sea-washed sand, its surface dotted here and there by clay patches scoured out by the recent storms. The tide was low and the surf could be heard pounding in the distance. In our path was a rusty tangled mass of barbed wire and iron stakes. Lifting Alex on to my shoulders I carefully threaded my way through these decaying defences to the firm untouched sand beyond.

Alex, set down on the sand with a murmured word of caution from me, ran shrieking with delighted anticipation towards the rollers ahead while I returned to the thoughts that had been milling around in my head. It was the end of 1945 and the war was over. After the first frenzied weeks of joyous delirium, when we had prayed our thanks for victory and survival, and grieved for those unable to share it, my mood had become more sombre and serious. The dramatic and almost overnight change in my day-to-day life was far more difficult to accept than I had at first anticipated. One cannot spend six years testing bombers and fighters continuously, with no break and in all weathers, without the manifestation of mental and physical scars. Like others I had for many years dreamed of the day when my wife Barbara, son Alex and I could live our lives in peace. I soon discovered that the transformation was not going to be as idyllic as I had envisaged.

My family had many commercial interests. Although not a farmer I did have substantial farm holdings. During the war the farms were tenanted in my absence and for a time I toyed with the idea of a tranquil postwar occupation in this capacity. Any serious aspirations I may have had in this direction however were soon quashed when I discovered that the myriad of legal documents which I thought were tenancy agreements, solemnly signed by both landlord and tenant, were useless. Security of tenure was inviolable by law.

It certainly did nothing to my sensibilities when I was advised by the Agricultural Executive Committee that farming was of such complexity to a person of my limited experience that they could not see their way clear to recommending an application for repossession of my own land on patriotic grounds alone, notwithstanding the fact that it had only been leased due to my wartime absence.

In all honesty I cannot say that Barbara and I grieved too much over this situation. At the time I felt a little bitterness but in retrospect I could understand a committee of farmers assuming that a pilot would be better suited to flying aircraft rather than looking after cows and growing corn. Although I had returned home to Lincolnshire I felt a stranger in my own county. I had left at the outbreak of war, like so many of my age, to tackle a strong and ruthless enemy. Eric, my youngest brother, had followed and joined the Royal Navy, only to be killed in action before his eighteenth birthday. Leslie, my other brother, wanted to become an air gunner. He was dissuaded from this and instead joined the 13th Light Field Ambulance. After living through traumatic experiences in the Western Desert he later had an horrific struggle for sheer survival against the Japanese in the Far East.

My introduction to war had certainly been more comfortable than that of my brothers. National recognition achieved through winning the 1938 King's Cup air race in the fastest time ever, coupled with the record flight from London to Cape Town and back the following year, stood me in good stead when I was faced with the momentous yet exciting decision on how best I could serve my country. But all this was history; now I had to consider the future for Barbara and Alex.

The most interesting but onerous prospects lay in the re-establishment of my family's large interest in holiday camps on the Lincolnshire coast, which had been occupied by our armed forces during the war. The future of these sites certainly offered enormous potential and excellent rewards, yet there were many problems to be considered, not least our emotions. We needed time for the flood of wartime memories to ebb from our minds. After a great deal of soul-searching Barbara and I reached a decision – we would go and live abroad, not for ever but certainly for a few years. Inwardly I was troubled that this move might prove to be a greater wrench than we anticipated. Despite the pressures and demands of my job at Vickers-Armstrongs, Barbara and I had been parted for only brief periods since our marriage in 1940, on the odd occasion when I was involved with aircraft carrier trials, gunnery and blind-flying courses. We loved our home and our decision to move was quite contrary to the plans we had made during the long dreary depressing years living in the Black Country. Logically, I should have stayed on with Vickers-Armstrongs and worked with Jeffrey Quill on the new and exciting generation of jet fighters then on the drawing board. Joe Smith, the chief designer and executive of Supermarine, had been very kind and considerate to me when the question of postwar test flying had been discussed. We had even demurred over the prospect of returning to live in the South of England, which in the past did not suit our health. Joe suggested that I undertake work on a part-time basis, flying down from Lincolnshire when required, but this was an idea I rejected without hesitation. I had survived several critical situations in the air only because I was very much in practice and on top of my job, both physically and mentally. Part-time flying and testing in such conditions, I reasoned, could only result in disaster. Had I been single the situation might have been different. I am quite sure I would have been more than happy to continue my harmonious association with the team I had worked with for so long at Supermarine. During the early part of the war I found the work with Jeffrey Quill, George Pickering and the friendly, informal yet efficient technical design team stimulating, exciting and enjoyable: a working environment that I missed so much when I subsequently took up my appointment as chief test pilot at the vast Castle Bromwich works. Another consideration was Barbara's peace of mind. Although she tried hard not to show it, Barbara suffered every new test flight. In the light of past experiences, some of them horrific and wounding, she had every reason to view a future of more test flying with some apprehension.

A sudden surge from a larger wave than usual rushed over Alex's little legs. The salt water splashed over his blue pantaloons and in his frantic efforts to leap backwards he fell over at my feet. Snapping back to reality I swept him into my arms and made tracks for home along the shore. Despite the blue sky and the glorious sunshine the beach was deserted. I pondered on what the beach would be like once the troops had left. Once the defences and mines were cleared families could revel once more on this wonderful part of the coastline, which so much blood had been spent to protect.

As I walked back with Alex chattering away, I saw a movement in the picturesque sand hills towards where I knew one of the Sutton-on-Sea golf course tees had been used as a wartime gun emplacement. This reminded me that here was another job I had yet to tackle. As owner of the course it was my responsibility to restore it after years of neglect and war damage.

Once Barbara and I had made up our minds to go abroad I started to look around for an acceptable occupation. The opportunity came unexpectedly out of the blue. Fred Miles, an old friend, telephoned to say that his company, Miles Aircraft, was about to form a new organisation in South Africa. Discussions towards this with General Mining & Finance Corporation in Johannesburg had already reached a fruitful stage and Albert Robinson, a member of the board, would be arriving in the UK that week. Fred explained to me what they had in mind and suggested a meeting, when further details could be discussed in confidence.

The idea appealed to me, as did the thought of living in South Africa, a part of the world I have always loved. In addition, I had known the Miles family since my early days of flying, and looked upon them with admiration and affection. Fred, with his disarming charm, was a worthy and likeable air race competitor. In addition his agile mind and prodigious energy enabled him to produce a constant flow of new and innovative aircraft that left other manufacturers spellbound. But for the phenomenal success of the Percival Mew Gull as a racing machine, I have no doubt that I would have turned to the Miles organisation to design and build me a suitable machine capable of beating the de Havilland Comet racer on a flight to the Cape and back. Miles did construct an aircraft for my 1935 King's Cup air race entry, the Miles M.2T Hawk Major G-ADNJ, but this proved a complete failure. The crankshaft of the new prototype Blackburn Cirrus Major engine broke over the Irish Channel during the race on September 6th, and in seconds a beautifully painted streamlined machine was reduced to a sodden, shattered mass of splintered spruce and plywood.

In addition to his versatility as an aircraft designer Fred Miles could sell his designs with such panache as to induce Percival and de Havilland to wince. For the 1935 King's Cup air race Miles had no fewer than 13 aircraft on the starting line, one of which, Miles M.3B Falcon Six G-ADLC flown by my old friend Major Tommy Rose, won. Fred Miles's wife, the equally charming Blossom, held perhaps a unique position in British aviation. Not only did she contribute to the overall design work but, as a brilliant mathematician, she worked on the stress calculations during the early days of the company.

On January 26th 1946 I flew down from Castle Bromwich to Woodley, where the Miles factory and offices were situated. I used the company's DH 89A Dominie R9546, one of the communications aircraft allocated to Vickers-Armstrongs by the Ministry of Aircraft Production. Although a slow biplane fitted with two de Havilland Gipsy Six Series II engines, the Dominie was completely reliable and a safe, easy machine to fly. Our Dominie had done sterling service, often in bad weather, ferrying my test pilots and their bulky parachutes from airfields where tested Spitfires and Lancasters had been dispersed. On the way over to Woodley I called in at Hatfield, the headquarters of the de Havilland Aircraft Company. There, Geoffrey de Havilland insisted on taking me to meet Hugh Buckingham, another old friend, in his open two-seat BMW sports car, to discuss the range of engines the de Havilland Engine Company intended to put into production.

As the factory of which Buckingham was in charge was at Stag Lane on the outskirts of North London, we did not return to Hatfield until after lunch. Although this delayed my meeting with Albert Robinson and the Miles directors, Robbie, as he was known to his friends, had already made up his mind about my appointment, and we got on well right from the start of our first meeting. Robbie had a politician's grasp of the spoken word and was the most able, perceptive and persuasive speaker I have ever met. I always thought he would become Prime Minister of South Africa – he was a Member of Parliament for a constituency of Johannesburg – but later on, as Sir Albert Robinson, he became High Commissioner for the Rhodesias & Nyasaland. When this folded up he became deeply involved with the Oppenheimer group.

At Woodley he clearly outlined his intentions. The new company was to be called Miles Aircraft South Africa Ltd and was to be partially financed by both Miles Aircraft UK and by Sir George Albu as Chairman of General Mining & Finance Corporation, Johannesburg. The board was to consist of Sir George as Chairman, Albert Robinson as Managing Director, Wing Commander Ian Hay (nephew to Albu) as Sales Director, and myself, for use of a better term, as he put it, Technical Director. I was to take up 3,000 shares on acceptance of the appointment and, if satisfied at the end of a two-year contract, I could take up a larger holding in the company and my position on the Board would be reviewed with the terms of my contract at that stage. My office was to be in the General Mining building in Johannesburg and I was invited to stay with the Albu family at their Parktown residence until I had bought a house and Barbara had arrived with Alex.

By the time this absorbing discussion had concluded the light outside was fading and Tommy Rose suggested that I should stay the night with him and his wife Billie. I, however, was impatient to return home and give Barbara my news. After thanking Tommy I rushed over to the Dominie, started the engines and took off for home. By this late hour RAF Strubby, my home aerodrome, was officially closed; there would be no personnel on the airfield and no lights. I reasoned that if I had difficulty in picking out Strubby then I would land on the beach at nearby Theddlethorpe where the tide rarely covered the beach. From past experience I knew the beach would reflect sufficient light from its yellow sand to enable me to pick out the coastline. The lamp inside the Dominie's small cockpit failed to work and so, having to rely upon my luminous compass, I put my map away. As the blackout had only recently been abolished I assumed that a small cluster of lights below were those of Bedford. When another cluster appeared ahead I was soon reassured and quite certain that they were the lights of Peterborough. When it began to rain I was unable to pick out any further landmarks until I sensed a tinge of lighter sky ahead that I knew must be the coastline. On reaching the coast I followed the dim outline of surf and, knowing every contour, was soon making a low pass over our house. I soon received a signal from Barbara as she flashed the garage light on and off, the code we used to tell me that she was on her way by car to pick me up from the airfield. I did not find Strubby easily. It had merged into the dark background of ploughed fields and trees and it was only when the lights of a passing car revealed the presence of a road that I eventually found the deeper shadows of the large, defunct hangars.

I switched on the aircraft's main nose beam. As I carefully circled overhead to position myself for the long runway the black gleaming reflection on the wet tarmac and hangar roofs played tricks with the shadows and indicated movement where I knew none existed. For a moment I was carried away into the past. Many times I had flown in to Strubby to witness Lancaster after Lancaster, heavy with their lethal loads, roar off into the night on a fateful mission from which many would not return.

After I landed I taxied slowly and carefully to the shelter of a large deserted hangar. When I switched off the engines there was silence, broken only by the steady drip, drip of water from the Dominie's wings. I waited patiently for the lights of Barbara's car to show. In the black silence of the night I could not help thinking of all those young men who, just a short time earlier, had occupied this very spot while bravely preparing for battle. It seemed somehow that their ghosts were with me that night; the memory of their departure will live with me forever.

CHAPTER 3

# "YOU'RE GOING TO HAVE A SORE ARSE BY THE TIME YOU GET THERE"

The tidying up of my affairs before departure for South Africa would have been impossible in the short time available had it not been for the energetic capabilities of Barbara. Some matters, particularly legal transactions, by the very nature of them could not be hurried. When war had broken out in September 1939, most peacetime activities stopped in their tracks, particularly when managers and operators left for active service. To suddenly turn round and pick up the loose ends after so many years was not easy.

Following further meetings with Fred and George Miles it was decided that it would be both practical and good sales publicity if I flew the company's first export Miles Messenger to Johannesburg. The Messenger was a single-engine low-wing monoplane capable of carrying a pilot and three passengers. Its main feature was its slow-flying characteristics. As Tommy Rose said to me after I told him of my plans: "My, but you're going to have a sore arse by the time you get there." Miles M.38 Messenger 2C G-AGUW took some time to prepare. When I flight-tested the aircraft on February 27th 1946 the cylinder-head temperatures of the 140 hp de Havilland Gipsy Major engine exceeded reasonable limits on full climbing power. As I did not relish a forced landing in some of the scorching high-altitude deserts I would need to cross, George Miles agreed with me that the engine cowling should be modified. It had been decided that I should take with me a ground engineer in addition to tools and spares. I would much rather have travelled alone but I had to agree that, once we started to demonstrate the Messenger, it would be unwise and impractical not to carry a good mechanic to keep the aircraft in first-class order. Time did not permit the opportunity of choosing one, but only days before the departure date I was told that a former Air Transport Auxiliary (ATA) flight engineer had applied for the job. His name was Salter and he told me subsequently that before he joined the ATA he was a point-to-point jockey. I later refrained from telling him I was sure he got on better with horses!

Parting from old friends is sad at the best of times. Those to whom I was about to say farewell had grown close to me during the past tense critical years when, at Castle Bromwich, we had lived amidst the sound of gunfire, falling bombs and the bloody mess of cleaning it all up. Almost the last of these friends that I saw was my Managing Director at Vickers-Armstrongs, Dickie Dickson and his wife Dorrie. When the time came to get up and go it seemed the end of an era. I felt shy and uncomfortable and I guess Dick felt the same, and I am sure Dorrie more so. On impulse, she grabbed me with a hug and a kiss and I hurried out before our emotions got the better

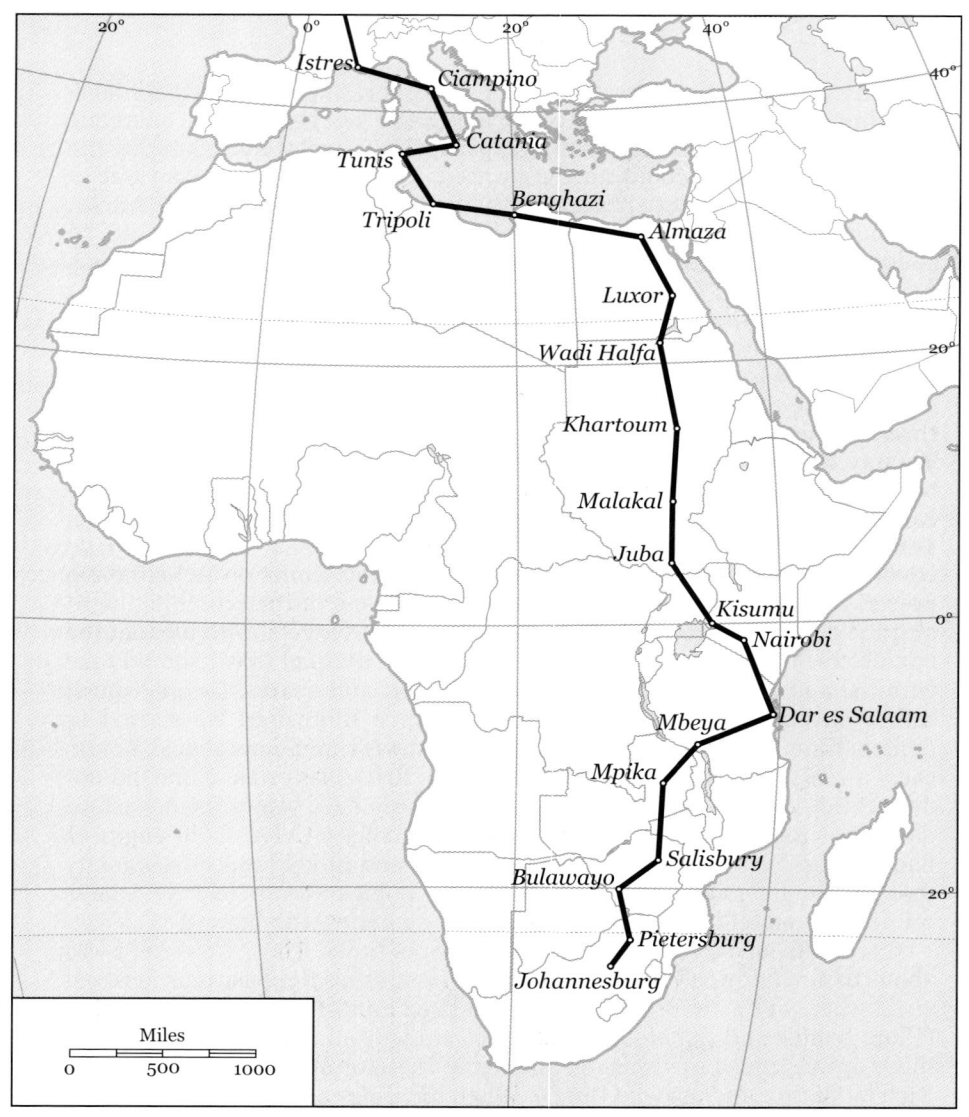

The author's route from Woodley to Johannesburg,
flown in Miles Messenger G-AGUW in March 1946.

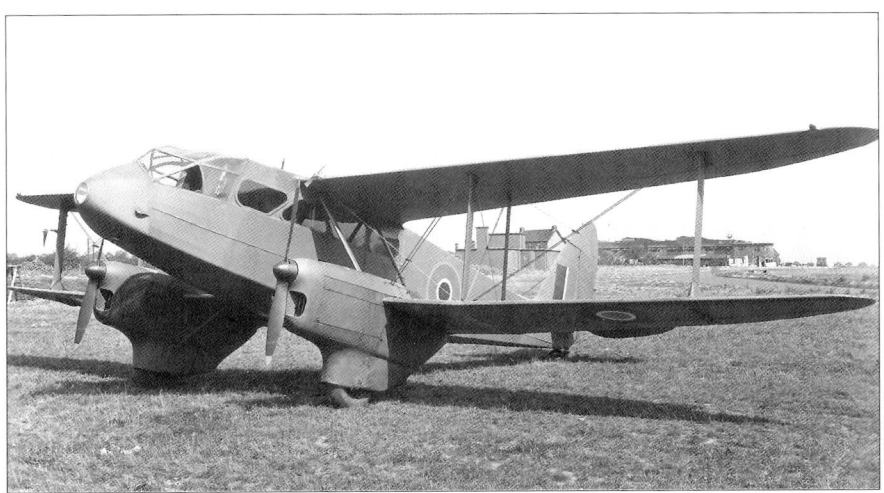

The RAF variant of the D.H. 89A Dragon Rapide, known as the Dominie, **above**, was used by the RAF as a navigation and radio trainer. Some also served as communications aircraft, while others did sterling service as hack or taxi aircraft for aircraft manufacturers. Although mostly used for ferrying test pilots from airfields where tested aircraft had been dispersed, Vickers-Armstrongs' Dominie R9546 was frequently flown by the author towards the end of the war. One of his last flights in R9546 was made in January 1946 to meet directors of Miles Aircraft Ltd shortly before taking up his employment with Miles Aircraft of South Africa (Pty.) Ltd.

The author and his wife Barbara pictured with Miles Messenger 2C G-AGUW at Woodley aerodrome in March 1946, shortly before the flight to South Africa. (Via Museum of Berkshire Aviation).

*An aerial view of Miles Aircraft's Woodley factory at Reading, taken on July 20, 1947 during a Miles "At Home" day for employees. The two aircraft parked in the foreground are Miles M.33 Monitors. Woodley closed as an active aerodrome in 1963.* (The Aeroplane photograph).

*Le Bourget airport pictured in March 1946, a few days after the author landed there in the Miles Messenger G-AGUW bound for Johannesburg. During the war the airport suffered heavily from land and air bombardment, and repair work was still in progress when this photograph was taken. A BOAC Douglas C-47A Dakota 3 stands on the apron.* (The Aeroplane photograph).

*Cairo's Almaza airfield seen from a BOAC Handley Page Halton in August 1946.* (The Aeroplane photograph).

*A Dakota and an RAF Avro York sweltering in the sun at Cairo's Almaza Airport in August 1946. In the distance at right can be seen a Misr-Airwork D.H. 86.* (The Aeroplane photograph).

*March 23, 1946. The author pictured after landing at Germiston, Johannesburg in the Miles Messenger 2C demonstrator G-AGUW on taking up his appointment with Miles Aircraft of South Africa (Pty.) Ltd. The flight out from Woodley, Reading was made in 15 days and totalled 82 flying hours.* (Author).

of us. Dick and Dorrie had suffered the tragic loss of a twelve-year-old son and both Barbara and I suspected that during those grim and demanding days at Castle Bromwich the Dicksons looked upon us as part of their family.

Salter and I eventually left Woodley aerodrome on the morning of March 8th 1946. Dad had a bout of asthma and was unable to motor down from Lincolnshire. I had said goodbye to Barbara and Alex in the hope that they would follow by airline soon. We had arranged to clear customs and immigration from Blackbushe, but the officials there refused to accept us and suggested we proceed to Croydon. There the officials were more co-operative and after a news camera team had taken shots from every angle we were allowed to proceed on our way. The Messenger of course was loaded to the brim. One of the four seats was replaced with an extra fuel tank and the rest of the cabin was packed with luggage, spares and equipment. I felt that it was rather like sitting on the back of a daddy-longlegs and I said to Salter that if we had to go uphill against a breeze we would slide down backwards. All I can say is that for a long time after we took off we had a good long look at people's gardens!

Le Bourget Airport at Paris had not yet recovered from the war and a small light aircraft was certainly not expected. Not that it mattered a great deal since customs and immigration facilities seemed non-existent. I parked alongside some American DC-3s and looked around for some form of control point. The Americans were too busy looking after themselves and others were too bewildered to bother with us.

The next day there was thick fog so I had the opportunity to see a little of grim reality. While the war was still in progress Barbara had visited France. She had a special pass to her old Château de Noirant home near Besançon, but she came back very saddened by what she had seen. The French, and Paris in particular, had suffered far more than we can comprehend under the heel of the German jackboot. For years the Gestapo had occupied the building next to the friend's house in which I stayed. Though the walls were thick this had not prevented the screams of the tortured from echoing down to the street below. I was shown the places and the means by which the French later settled old scores when the tide did at last turn. No quarter was given, no questions were asked.

The weather in Paris remained foggy and bitterly cold and it was not until March 11th that we were able to get away. The Messenger was certainly no Spitfire, and as I knew that the Massif Central was obscured in snow and cloud and was blocking our way, I lost little time in coaxing her into a climb for altitude. During the climb we picked up a great deal of ice and the machine became nose-heavy and oscillated badly as the triple fins and rudders collected more than their fair share. It was not that the cloud was unduly thick, but the slow rate of climb kept me in it longer than I had expected. Eventually we broke through into brilliant sunshine and before long were clipping over the tops of snow-covered mountains before making a shallow dive to the enormous airfield at Istres, Marseille. There, stacks of war stores and equipment covered every spare metre of space, while the runways and aprons were lined with American military aircraft of all types. By landing almost at the control tower, rather than on the main runway that seemed miles away, we caused a minor sensation. The officer in charge was somewhat nonplussed as to how he should deal with a civilian aircraft, especially when I asked for what to him was a minuscule quantity of low octane fuel.

Because the French officials were apathetic and useless we did not clear customs or immigration. The moment the Americans had refuelled us, amidst great guffaws and much hilarity, we proceeded once more on our way towards Italy.

I soon realised that we should not reach Rome before dark. The weather was now wonderful after the harshness of northern Europe and it was not long before we were struggling out of the winter clothes we had worn since leaving home. The lights of Rome led us in from the sea and we made for the flare path of Ciampino on the southern outskirts of the city. I had arranged to meet General Vittorio, an old friend of Barbara's, that evening. He had been very proud of the fact that his family had commanded a crack cavalry regiment for three generations. His own experience of war had started at the age of 14; his father had taken him into the trenches during the Battle of Caporetto and he witnessed one of the last cavalry charges in modern war, between the Austrians and his father's old regiment. The General showed me a faded, once colourful busby and a sabre, which he had picked up from the field of battle after it was all over. He was a little ill at ease and in order to make conversation I asked him, over our evening meal, if he had experienced a bad war. He paused and replied somewhat stiffly: "I was at Tobruk."

The next day we set course for the flight along the Italian coast to Sicily. The sea crossing to Tunis was warm and pleasant, but uneventful and slow. After a night's rest in the army barracks at Tunis we took off at first light on March 13th for Tripoli. When we reached the vast expanse of open desert I could not refrain from easing back the throttle and slowly weaving from side to side at zero feet to view what lay around. The scene reminded me of the battlefields of Verdun over which I had flown with my father so many years earlier. True, there were no trenches or ramparts, but here over this Libyan wilderness was an enormous panorama strewn with the destructive impedimenta of war, stretching to the horizon and beyond. Tyre and caterpillar tracks criss-crossed everywhere, looking as though they had been made yesterday. Lorries, tanks, gun-carriers, burnt out depots and crashed aircraft, all turning red with rust, littered the landscape. As I looked down at the myriad of tracks and debris I marvelled that so much more had not been obliterated by the wind and sand, and wondered why the enterprising Arabs had not yet cleared this litter of war. As we flew along a Messerschmitt Bf.109 came into view on my right – not in the air but lying on its belly, undamaged below us. For a moment I was sorely tempted to land alongside. What would I find in the cockpit – a young German, his life surrendered in its prime for the Fatherland? Sombre reflection brought to mind a mental picture of how the battle must have raged below. So many young men, on both sides, all fighting for what they believed was right. So many dead, maimed and wounded – for what?

I was suddenly conscious of the incongruous noise of my engine over this scene where, not long ago, thousands were locked together in a death grip from which only a lucky few would survive the scars of war. I slowly eased the throttle forward, turned back on to course and climbed away from this poignant reminder of an era that had altered all our lives.

So absorbed had I been with this fascinating experience that I had not noticed the time. A glance at my watch showed that we had fallen behind schedule. I said to Salter, who had been equally mesmerised by the scene below, that we would push on hard to Benghazi and have a clean up and a meal before carrying on through the night to Cairo.

RAF personnel, whose only interest was to get the hell out of the place and return home, then occupied Benghazi. After we landed I left Salter to refuel the Messenger while I tried to obtain some Met. information. I remembered the risk of ground fog over the Nile at this time of year and we were without radio or blind-flying aids beyond a turn & bank indicator. When I returned to the aircraft, I saw to my consternation one of the RAF mechanics walking along the fragile wing of the Messenger with a fuel hose in his hands while Salter looked on, unmoved.

"Get off that wing, you bloody idiot," I shouted, rushing up in such a threatening manner that the mechanic leapt wildly from the wing to the ground.

"I'm sorry, sir," he said, when he had collected himself, "we always used to fill up Beaufighters this way."

I felt a little ashamed of my outburst of temper and replied: "I know, I am sorry I barked like that but this is a plywood-covered wing, thin as tissue paper and you are lucky that you did not put your foot right through it." Then, turning to the uncomfortable-looking Salter, I said acidly: "You are the one to blame, why the hell do you think I left you here?"

We parked the Messenger on the tarmac apron under the hangar lights and strolled across to the RAF mess for a shower and a somewhat meagre meal. When we had finished we stepped outside. The sky had taken on that deep purple glow that only the desert seems to provide and the air felt soft and soothing after the enervating heat of the day. Under the lights of the hangar I checked the compass bearings from my map. We had neither lights nor a battery on the Messenger and, strictly speaking, what I was about to do contravened all air navigation rules. But in that immediate postwar atmosphere over Libya and Egypt no one was likely to be unduly bothered by a little infringement such as this. Assured from an earlier inspection that the way ahead was clear, I opened the throttle and the Messenger was airborne before we had left the tarmac; then we set course for the aerodrome at Almaza.

I have never been in love with Cairo but I could not help a feeling of fascination creep over me as I watched the soft glow that threw long shadows around the Sphinx and the pyramids. With the crowded River Nile flowing like a green necklace through the desert, the almost immobile *dhows* and slow-moving camels conjured up visions right out of the Bible.

The sleepy-eyed Egyptians were hopelessly helpful and very excited to see the first British private aeroplane from the United Kingdom since before the war. Because everyone was asking questions and giving unwanted advice we had great difficulty in getting away. One fat pompous gentleman lectured me for ages on the dangers of flying across Egypt and the Sudan. Without being rude I could not get away from him as he had me pinned against the Messenger's wing and the fuselage. Someone, guessing my plight, came up and whispered something in the man's ear.

The effect was quite remarkable. The fat man almost kissed me in his excitement. "I am so sorry, why did you not tell me who you are? If only I had known how many times you have crossed the desert." And so he rambled on.

We spent the next day in Luxor where we not only had time to tour the sights but the opportunity to give the Messenger a careful inspection and complete a 50-hour schedule on the Gipsy engine.

It was now March 16th and with the desert warming up we made Khartoum after a brief stop at Wadi Halfa. I think I could have reached Khartoum to Juba direct in one flight but I had great respect for that forbidding swamp, the sudd. I decided to call in at Malakal in order to top up our tanks, including an auxiliary that we carried on the back seat. After a night's stop at Juba listening to the whinges of the bored and frustrated RAF men awaiting demobilisation, we left that austere lonely spot for a protracted climb over the heights to reach Nairobi.

To my surprise and delight the first person to meet us on landing at Nairobi was Bill Knoulden, the Commanding Officer at Castle Bromwich at the time I was appointed chief test pilot there in June 1940. He and his wife gave us a very warm welcome and insisted that I stayed with them in their charming house on the outskirts of the city.

Later the next day there was a phone call from an excited Salter saying that the Messenger was breaking up structurally and that as he had not sufficient tools and equipment to carry out a major repair, I had better get over there right away. Bill quickly ran me over to the airfield in his car, and when I carefully examined the underbelly of the Messenger I could see that, though a panel of thin plywood had split longitudinally, fortunately it was

*"Lorries, tanks, gun-carriers, burnt out depots and crashed aircraft, all turning red with rust, littered the landscape."*
(Painting of Miles M.38 Messenger 2C G-AGUW by Michael Turner).

**Above,** *Miles Messenger 2C G-AGUW, flown from Woodley to Johannesburg by the author, having its compass swung shortly after its arrival at Germiston in March 1946.*

**Right,** *view of Johannesburg taken from the right-hand seat of Miles Messenger G-AGUW during a flight from Germiston in March 1946.*

**Below,** *another view of G-AGUW pictured at Germiston shortly after its arrival in March 1946.* (Ron Moulton photographs).

not in a stress area. As I had promised Albert Robinson I would arrive in Johannesburg in time for the Rand Show I told Salter to cover the split with doped fabric but not to bother with the paintwork. He was not very happy about this but fortunately the chief engineer to East African Airways had arrived, at Bill's request, and quickly confirmed my own views.

On our way southwards I had been invited to visit the British Director of Civil Aviation at Dar es Salaam in Tanganyika, who was interested in acquiring an aircraft for use in his enormous territory. Rowe, the Director, was a correct, polite and well-mannered civil servant but his aide, I remember, was an arrogant and offensive individual who bullied and kicked the natives around in a manner that made my blood boil. It was all I could do to restrain myself from interference.

On March 20th we left the picturesque tropical setting of Dar es Salaam for Mbeya, a lonely place in the mountains where, during my survey flight in the Vega Gull for the Cape record attempt with my father, I had shown the first signs of malaria that I had picked up at Point Noire and which was to put me in hospital in Khartoum. Mbeya had, however, the redeeming feature of a long tarmac runway – unusual for any airstrip in Africa in those early days. Although Mbeya is 5,000 ft above sea level and it was mid-day and hot, I had no qualms about the take-off performance of the Messenger under such conditions. Nevertheless I always used the maximum run available on any take-off, and it was as well that I did so now. I had naturally expected a great drop in performance taking off in such high temperatures and at such altitude, but I was somewhat shaken and not prepared for what happened next.

After opening the throttle the Messenger lifted off quite early and easily, but refused to climb. Reasoning that the flaps were inducing too much drag I raised them to the closed position, to no avail. We still hung in the air at about 40 m.p.h and I realised that we were sitting on a cushion of air between the aircraft and the ground. Unfortunately the comparatively good take-off had misled me into thinking that I could gather sufficient speed before the end of the runway. In this I was sadly mistaken. We were now off the runway with the engine giving full power, but so low that a rock or a bush in our path would have brought us down to disaster. Salter clutched the seat in silence, his face white and tense. A solid-looking boulder slid by inches beneath the port wing as I delicately eased the machine over to manoeuvre between a sisal plant on one wingtip and a *mapani* tree on the other. I heard Salter suck in his breath and murmur, "Christ!"

For my part I was tense with concentration. I knew what I had to do, if only I had the time in which to do it. I prayed for a thermal that would give me the few feet of lift I needed, or a slight downward gradient that would allow a little additional speed to be picked up. During this gentle balancing act on the cushion of air I had worked my way a little to the south-east of the airfield, where the ground appeared to fall slightly away. This time I was in luck. Not only did the machine start to pick up a little speed, we crossed a healthy thermal that allowed me to alter the dangerous angle of attack that was inducing so much drag. I was able to begin a steady climb and the danger passed. Salter and I sank back in our seats and looked at each other with a great sigh of relief.

At Mpika we refuelled quickly as I was anxious to reach Salisbury before nightfall, but as we taxied to the airfield boundary the Gipsy engine suddenly lost power and, for no apparent reason, stopped. My first thought was that it must be water in the petrol, or a blocked fuel line. Just as we started to check things out, however, I realised the problem was a vapour lock, a common occurrence in very hot conditions at high altitude, and a hazard so well-known to pioneer fliers in these regions that many of them would not fly without having a special pressure pump with which to clear the fuel lines. By the time we had cured the problem it was too late to continue and so we decided to stay the night.

The next morning we crossed the Zambesi so early that the animals were still at their watering holes. At our approach hippo, buck, elephant, crocodile, buffalo and numerous other animals rushed into the jungle or undergrowth. At Salisbury we were given a warm welcome and I was sorry we had to push on so quickly to Bulawayo. My take-off from Salisbury was not as bad as we had experienced at Mbeya but it was poor enough to remind me that I must fit the fine-pitch propeller we had strapped inside the fuselage.

The Rhodesians at Bulawayo were wonderful people and we felt happy and at home. So far the Messenger had made quite a good impression but there were several important points that did much to allay a quick sale. Firstly, it was made of wood, which is not the best material for aircraft in a harsh climate such as that of Africa. Secondly, it was expensive when comparable American machines were cheaper. Thirdly, and worst of all, we could not give early delivery.

Fifteen days after leaving Woodley aerodrome we arrived at the Rand Airport precisely on schedule on March 23rd, to a tremendous welcome that had been arranged by Robbie. After I had met Sir George Albu and his wife Betty, Mary Robinson, Ian and Annette Hay and dozens of local people, I attended a large press conference. The welcome could not have been warmer; I liked Sir George and Betty Albu immediately and as far as Ian Hay is concerned I can say only that he is still one of my closest friends more than 55 years later.

Mary and Robbie Robinson did all they could to help me settle and adjust to the new life. George and Betty Albu were also very considerate friends and hosts. Their marvellous home in Parktown reminded me of the stately stone houses to be found in the North of England – solid and well-built. My first impressions of Johannesburg, after six dreary years of war in England, led me to think it was indeed the Garden of Eden. My first priority was to find a suitable home in readiness for Barbara and Alex, whom I expected to arrive from England any day. Although I enjoyed staying with the Albu family it was not long before I began to see cracks in the gilt and glitter of this raucous city, but I decided to keep my opinions to myself until I could discuss the future with Barbara.

I was soon to learn that although many South Africans were pro-British I was constantly up against a large hardcore of enthusiasts who only had time for American aircraft, cars and many other good products produced by this vigorous and commercially aggressive country. I had to admit that many of their reasons were perfectly valid but, as a loyal and patriotic Briton, I had to push these to one side and work flat out to win every commercial battle that I could. Under normal circumstances I would not have minded an arduous struggle to compete in a tough and strange land. Unknowingly, perhaps, I had chosen a huge sprawling cosmopolitan city that during the war and immediate postwar years had become vulgar with wealth and burdened with corruption and violence. The city now attracted the scum of the earth and a constant influx of the upper echelons of society in seemingly equal proportions. I was lucky with my friends. Ian Hay, who had been a Royal Air Force Wing Commander, had been educated at Rugby and Cambridge and, as a member of one of the oldest and most respected families in South Africa, he realised more than most how disenchanted I was becoming. Inwardly I knew that Ian felt much the same way, but he was loyal to his friends and family. Nevertheless, I was contracted for two years and, though I may have been carried away by the enthusiasm of Robbie and George, there was a great deal to be done and I entered into the spirit of the job with vigour and enthusiasm.

My first task on arrival at Johannesburg was to establish an aircraft service organisation. On reflection this turned out to be too large and elaborate for the amount of business that was available at the time. There is little doubt that, had we had suitable aircraft ready to sell, and had we been able to assure early delivery, we could have sold a sufficient number of aircraft in the whole of South Africa to make the organisation a viable proposition. As it was, I flew the Messenger everywhere. The reception it received, on the whole, was enthusiastic, but you cannot sell goods on a promise of delivery when your competitors can offer something as good, if not better, that is already on the dockside waiting to be collected by the customer. Fortunately General Mining & Finance, although primarily a gold mining concern, was involved in textiles, breweries, farming and the import and export of a large range of products. There was always an atmosphere of excitement in the office that Robbie, Ian and I shared and there was always the exhilaration of some new aircraft sales prospect in Walvis Bay, Angola, the Belgian Congo or Mozambique etc.

Sir George Albu was a great public benefactor and the first such organisation with which he became associated was "The People of Britain

Fund". In early April 1946 I took Edsel Jonnsen, the fund's organiser, and C.S. Maclean, Director and Mining Engineer of our own group, on a long and detailed tour of the Union in the Messenger. The tour went to schedule and, though it was successful from the point of view of the Fund, my aircraft order book remained empty.

When not travelling my weekends with the Albu family did much to ease my frustration and impatience over the fact that Barbara had not yet managed to obtain a passage out from England. Mostly we would go out to their larger farm at Pienards River. The large ranch-type house was well set back in the bush amidst the wildlife. As you approached the place along a winding dusty track the captivating scene of attractive *rondavel* units fanning out from the main house met you. I received several other invitations to stay with others, but owing to the great distances involved in many instances I had to choose with care. Whenever the opportunity arose I did however enjoy going up to Southern Rhodesia with Col. Lord Ellis Robbins. He was an early member of the British South Africa Company and knew all the pioneers who had struggled and fought to make Northern and Southern Rhodesia what they had become. It was they who had provided the key to the prosperity and advantages offered to blacks and whites alike. I always found the Rhodesians easy to get on with and made friends immediately wherever I went. Some of these were men in their seventies and eighties, like Sir Francis Newton. Despite their advancing years, their clarity of thought and their descriptions of those early days, in a land that seemed to offer nothing but heat, toil and fear of illness, made one realise what had been achieved in such a short time. And what a contrast it had provided when compared with the standard of life given to the coloured population in a place like Johannesburg.

# Log of flight from Woodley to Germiston,
## March 8th–23rd 1946 in Miles Messenger G-AGUW

| Date | From | To | Time | | Remarks |
|------|------|-----|----|----|---------|
| March 8 | Woodley | Blackbushe | | 10 | |
| " | Blackbushe | Croydon | | 20 | Customs |
| " | Croydon | Le Bourget | 1 | 52 | |
| March 11 | Le Bourget | Istres | 4 | 25 | |
| " | Istres | Ciampino | 4 | 37 | |
| March 12 | Ciampino | Catania | 3 | 51 | |
| " | Catania | Tunis | 2 | 50 | |
| March 13 | Tunis | Tripoli | 4 | 20 | |
| " | Tripoli | Benghazi | 5 | 10 | |
| March 14 | Benghazi | Almaza | 6 | 15 | |
| " | Almaza | Luxor | 3 | 25 | |
| March 16 | Luxor | Wadi Halfa | 3 | 00 | |
| " | Wadi Halfa | Khartoum | 4 | 50 | |
| March 17 | Khartoum | Malakal | 3 | 40 | |
| " | Malakal | Juba | 3 | 15 | |
| March 18 | Juba | Kisumu | 5 | 00 | |
| " | Kisumu | Nairobi | 1 | 50 | |
| March 19 | Nairobi | Dar es Salaam | 4 | 00 | |
| " | Dar es Salaam | Local | | 45 | Demonstration |
| March 20 | Dar es Salaam | Mbeya | 4 | 00 | |
| " | Mbeya | Mpika | 2 | 25 | |
| March 21 | Mpika | Salisbury | 4 | 00 | |
| " | Salisbury | Bulawayo | 2 | 25 | |
| March 22 | Bulawayo | Local | 1 | 00 | Demonstration |
| March 23 | Bulawayo | Johannes-burg | 5 | 00 | via Pietersburg |
| | | | **Total flying time 82 15** | | |

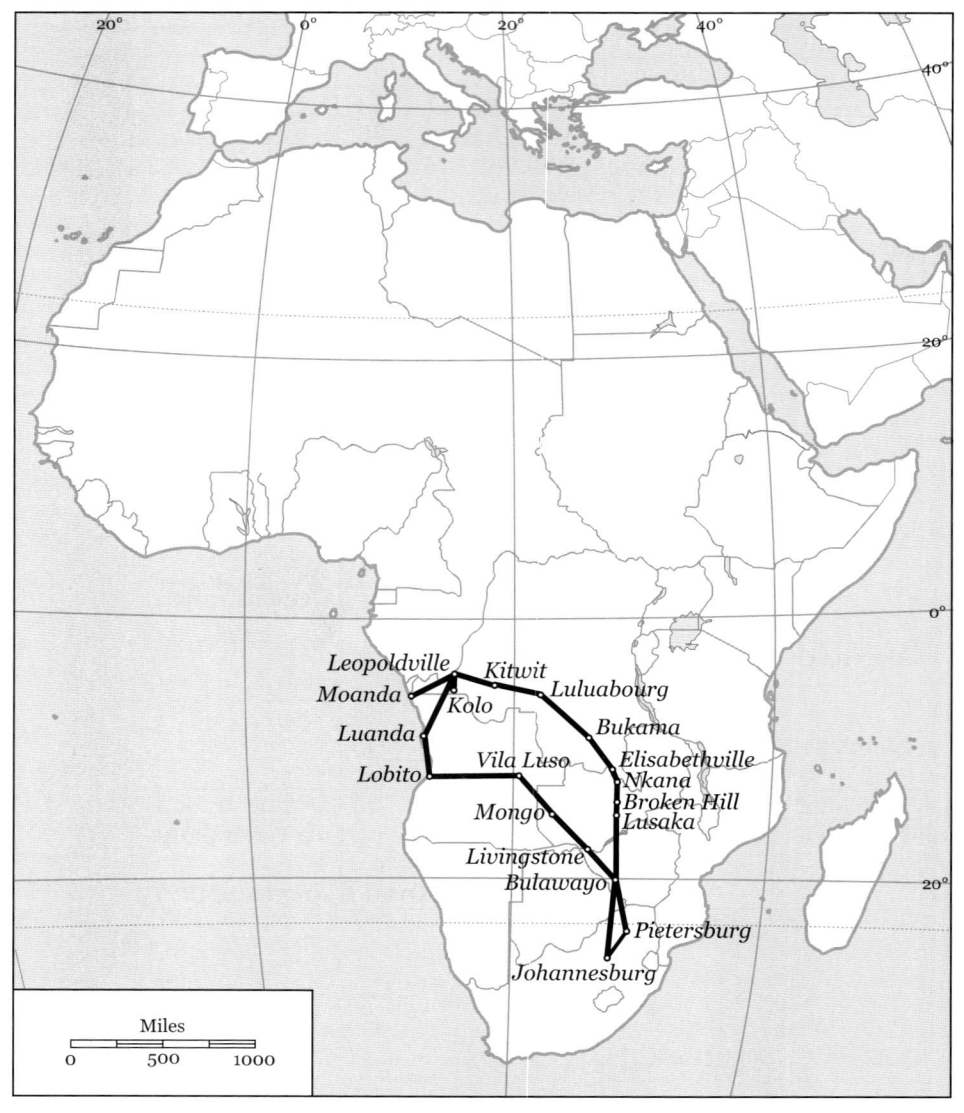

The route of the author's sales tour,
flown in Miles Messenger G-AGUW from Johannesburg in June 1946.

CHAPTER 4

# UNITED

On my return from one of these visits I strode into my office in high spirits. On opening a letter from Barbara my morale sank to its lowest depths: I read that she was still unable to obtain a passage out to South Africa. It was now three months since we had parted and as each week passed I waited expectantly for good news but, other than the occasional telephone call and the regular letters – filled with the problems of living in early post-war Britain – my hopes were beginning to sink. Inwardly I felt this was the most miserable period of my life. I was also incensed because I had met many people with priorities much lower than those of Barbara who had, by whatever means, obtained a seat with the overcrowded airlines.

I have always tried to avoid string-pulling but now I felt angry and bitter, so irately I telephoned the managing director of an airline booking company with whom we did considerable business, and coldly pointed out to him the facts of life. After telephoning his London office he confirmed that Barbara and Alex would be booked on a Pan American Lockheed Constellation scheduled to leave Heathrow for Leopoldville on June 20th to connect with the South African Airways service for Johannesburg. Thrilled and excited with the news, I went about my work with renewed vigour.

As the date for their departure drew nearer a strange feeling of anxiety crept over me. I had a hunch that something was going to go wrong. Notwithstanding the confirmation I had received from London I rang up South African Airways to check that the reservations were in order at Leopoldville. They could not help, saying they would not have an up-to-date passenger list until the day of departure. It so happened that we had decided at a recent board meeting to embark upon a sales survey of the Congo and Angola. Telling Ian Hay of my fears, we then decided to alter the dates and arrange our visit to coincide with the SAA Constellation's time of arrival at Leopoldville.

Early on the morning of June 10th 1946 we loaded the little Messenger with samples of all the various products we were importing, or upon which we had franchise rights, and set off for Bulawayo and Livingstone *en route* for Angola. From Livingstone we were going to leave the beaten track for uncharted territory to savour the trip in a spirit of adventure. Our schedule called for the flight from Livingstone to the west coast of Africa to be made in a single day. With the Messenger's low speed and poor range this necessitated a very early start and some night flying.

We arrived safely at Livingstone, via Bulawayo, that night after 6 hr 15 min in the air. Livingstone was then a small grass airfield in an attractive setting with a modern hotel and the ever-spuming Victoria Falls close by. There was little or no flying control and of course landing lights were unheard of. Next day we hired a car from our hotel and at 4 am set off with a native driver for the unattended airfield, both Ian and I wondering if we were doing the right thing. There was no moon and the night was as black as pitch. On arrival at the field I took over from the driver and positioned the car so that the headlights shone down the airstrip, instructing him not to move the car until the sound of our engine had died away.

We took off without incident and set course for Mongo, Ian navigating to leave me free to concentrate on the flying. Without cockpit lighting and only a small compass and turn and bank indicator, there was no time for me to relax. What made it additionally difficult at first was that, surprisingly, there was no visible horizon and I had to rely on the stars to navigate. Mongo, an almost unheard-of dot on the map, was perched on the edge of a low ridge overlooking the swamps of the River Zambesi, its sprawling tributaries winding their way across Barotseland into the high ground of Angola. I said to Ian: "My God, we can't afford to miss Mongo."

It was still dark and Ian had no means of knowing, as I did, what lay beneath us. It was unpleasant to say the least and we had insufficient fuel to go elsewhere. As we flew on it seemed to us both that dawn was a long time coming, and it was only when we chanced to look back that we saw the first streaks of lightening sky in the east, whilst ahead it was still as black as ink. We had calculated that we would strike Mongo at first light, but when eventually we could see the ground there was not a solitary fix from which we could derive some comfort. Below us were the mushy-looking green swamps and the black areas of the flooded land, broken by isolated patches of higher ground on which herds of wildebeest scattered as we approached. There was no high ground of any significance in sight and certainly nothing high enough to accommodate an airstrip. After taking the map from Ian I said: "If our time is correct there is only one thing that can have happened; we have had a tailwind and we have overshot."

We turned back on an exact reciprocal course and within minutes could see the tiny outpost of Mongo and a Union Jack languidly hanging from a crooked flagpost on the narrow dirt track that served as the airstrip. The little mound on which the strip was placed stood as a silent haven amidst the forbidding swamps; a sole thatched dwelling the only evidence of humanity.

As we touched down after a flight of a little more than two hours the District Commissioner came out to greet us, a solitary figure in white, happy at the sight of such unexpected visitors. Whenever I think of the old British Empire and its history I picture that lonely man in his immaculate safari gear, doing his duty in isolation and discomfort.

The next leg of our flight was to Vila Luso in Angola. After thanking the Commissioner for his kindness and help we quickly proceeded on our way. Not long after we had settled down to our cruising level of 6,000 ft the Gipsy engine began to misfire. By now we had left the swamps behind and I searched for a suitable track near a village upon which we could put down. Ian said nothing but, as he said afterwards, he thought plenty! All I could think of was that we were going to have a mighty long walk and that I had only six bullets in my automatic. The engine continued to run rough and misfire for about half an hour whilst we scanned the uninviting terrain below then, suddenly, it cleared itself and continued to run as smooth as a sewing machine. I remarked to Ian that the problem could have been plugs or magneto and that we would have to check them on landing.

We saw Vila Luso almost spot on track. On landing the little grass airstrip was soon crowded with primitive natives and scruffy-looking Portuguese, all milling around the Messenger as though no one had landed there before. Ian remarked what a villainous lot they all looked. Though undoubtedly true I have always had a very soft spot for any Portuguese, as they once saved my life at Mossamedes during my record-breaking return flight to the Cape. I also jokingly reminded Ian that the Portuguese were Britain's oldest allies.

At Vila Luso everyone was extremely friendly. After a short wait in the blazing sun that almost fried us alive, the lorry with petrol aboard arrived. Once fuelled up we were soon able to clamber aboard and ease the burning soles of our feet, then with all vents and windows open we took off and climbed towards cooler air.

Our night stop at Lobito, a tiny Angolan village right on the Atlantic beach, was soothingly pleasant. Ian and I frolicked in the waves, washing away the sweat of more than nine hours flying that day, and then enjoyed a simple meal whilst watching the burning sun sink slowly over the water.

The next morning, on June 12th, we left Lobito and flew along the deserted coast to the small town of Luanda. Here we stopped to negotiate some business with the Portuguese internal airline based there. Though they were very pleased to see us they were not in the market for anything we had to offer. We moved on to Leopoldville and landed on what must have been one of the largest and best airports in Africa at that time. The enormous concrete runways made the Messenger appear ridiculous as we taxied towards an enormous expanse of concrete in front of the control tower. The whole place seemed to be devoid of either aircraft or personnel. After booking into a clean and presentable hotel my first task was to check Barbara's reservations with Pan American and South African Airways. My earlier hunch had been correct: I was livid to discover that although she was due on the 20th as arranged, South African Airways could not get a connecting flight to Johannesburg until the following week, though they did have a single spare seat on the flight leaving the day before she was due to arrive! Ian and I chewed over the problem and decided that he would take the SAA seat back to Johannesburg while I would wait and bring Barbara and Alex along in the Messenger.

In the meantime we had a great deal to keep us busy. Our first visit out into the jungle surrounding Leopoldville was to a plantation a little more than 100 miles to the south. Our destination was an estate named Kolo, established by a Belgian family by the name of van Lancker. At the time I met Mr van Lancker Snr he was more than seventy years of age and had a large family. As a young man he had trekked on foot through the virgin jungle, with everything he possessed on the heads of twelve natives, to this spot on which he had chosen to carve an empire for himself.

We landed on a grass airstrip that ran close to van Lancker's solid and substantial residence. As we climbed out of the Messenger his sons, daughters-in-law and grandchildren greeted us; we were made most welcome and they insisted that we come in for a wash and a meal before being shown around this remarkable place. I liked the old man and admired him for what he had achieved in his lifetime. He had his own railway and siding, running from Leopoldville – a rare thing in this savage country. He had put down enormous kernel plantations and with his own laboratories crushed and purified his own oil. There were huge areas of sisal from which he made numerous grades of rope. On the land that he had been able to clear were thousands of head of cattle and the whole organisation was thriving with activity. I am not sure how many natives he employed but they were all housed in brick-built dwellings with a Catholic and Protestant church to serve both denominations. Van Lancker talked about his early struggles, when to survive was an achievement in itself. He had to fight to protect his interests and once, when his white overseer was missing, he went out armed with a few trusty natives to find him. They found the overseer, after driving off cannibals, pegged to the ground and about to be carved up and roasted over a large fire.

When, later, I flew van Lancker in the Messenger he was very impressed. He said that he was getting too old for fast machines and the Messenger was safe and child's play to fly. He was not slow to point out however that this country was extremely dangerous terrain over which to fly and that he would prefer to have a twin-engined aircraft. By this time Miles had introduced the twin-engined Gemini and when we reluctantly left Kolo we promised to bring the Gemini over once we received the first demonstrator.

Our next visit was to Moanda on the mouth of the Congo. The flight, mainly along this mighty river, was a sight almost hypnotic to behold. Tempestuous surging water ceaselessly cascades over the gigantic rocks as the river plunges its forceful passage through the high jungle trees on its journey to the Atlantic. While flying low over the river we had to take care not to fly into the fine bird nets ingeniously strung across from the tall branches either side by the natives.

Moanda was the private domain of another Belgian, Albert Fischer. It was a delightful spot with the owner's bungalow perched on top of low cliffs overlooking a clean narrow beach over which the Atlantic waves pounded.

The airstrip extended up to the bungalow and featured a well-thatched and ventilated hangar. Fischer was a big, tough, jovial man of tremendous character. He had an impish sense of humour and in many ways reminded me of my own father. Immensely wealthy, he bought cars, lorries and aeroplanes like some people buy packets of tea. He owned large tracts of jungle, chosen for their prime timber, and during the war he had driven some hard bargains with the Americans. A man of his word, he expected other people to keep theirs. He was also very useful with a rifle and his gun-bearers knew that he could put a bullet between the eyes of man or beast at up to 200 yards. This was certainly a good prognosis for peace should any of the locals have other ideas. Fischer and I became firm friends immediately; I liked his cavalier attitude to life in a country that did not accept weaklings. He had created a lifestyle in darkest Africa that I would previously have thought impossible. Although the Moanda property was not his main house it was luxurious in a very practical way and the accommodation provided for his guests was to the same standard.

Thus it was that I needed no persuading to accept Fischer's invitation to bring Barbara and Alex out for a visit when the opportunity arose. He did at the same time warn me not to treat the jungle lightly. A forced landing of any sort literally meant sudden death, and a slow and painful one at that. As Fischer said: "The only things that will get to you will be the ants, and they'll smell you a mile off, and when they find you they'll pick your bones dry."

By that time I had seen enough of that wet stinking forest, as vast as an ocean, to know that Fischer spoke the truth. As a result I became more and more apprehensive of the journey I was soon to face taking Barbara and Alex to Johannesburg. We left Kolo promising to meet again, when the Messenger and Gemini Fischer had ordered were ready for delivery.

Ian Hay caught his flight as arranged and I waited impatiently for the Pan American Constellation to arrive from London. When at last it did come into sight I prayed that Barbara and Alex would be aboard and that there had been no last minute foul-up. I waited tensely at the barriers. Then, as the passengers came slowly down the gangway I saw Barbara, tired and travel-stained, descending with Alex in her arms. No longer able to restrain myself I brushed aside the protesting officials and forced my way up the gangway steps and took Alex from Barbara's arms. He had his arms around my neck before Barbara was aware that I was beside her, and then she clutched my arm in surprise.

As we drove quickly through Leopoldville to our hotel Alex chattered away whilst Barbara and I were silent, just happy to be in each other's company once more. The contented bliss, as we sat down to our evening meal after a cool and reviving shower, was something that I cannot adequately put into words. Though we had been parted as a family for four months it had seemed more like a lifetime. After a good night we were all ready the next morning for the long journey ahead.

Though the morning of June 22nd was fine as we took off and climbed on to course, I took every moment with deliberation, taking every possible precaution, and never relaxed even for a second. The first leg of the long journey was over a sea of virgin jungle to Kitwit. The small landing strip was carved from the ridge of a gentle rise and could be easily missed. I purposely kept a very accurate time check, intending to turn back if I did not sight the airstrip first time. We had no difficulty in finding the place, for the visibility was good. On landing came the tedious task of pumping fuel from a forty-gallon drum with just one native to help. We took off and headed for Luluabourg and again were faced with a forbidding green carpet below us. The seemingly limitless expanse of jungle gave way to broken countryside as we approached the small but attractive settlement, and I was able to relax for the first time.

I liked Luluabourg. We stayed in a small thatched ranch-type bungalow that was both clean and comfortable. After a refreshing shower the three of us sat down to a good but simple meal. Afterwards we put Alex safely under the mosquito netting; Barbara and I were soon to follow.

My spirits dropped a little the next morning as the weather had changed, with low cloud and mist shrouding the trees nearby. I did not like the look of it but realised that in this part of the world such weather was typical. We might have to wait for weeks for perfect conditions. I waited an hour and then as the sky appeared to lighten I decided to see what it was like. As I had half expected, by the time we had settled on to the correct height and course, the heat of the rising sun broke up the dense cloud into patches and enabled us to see once again the unbroken jungle below. There was not a trace of track or village visible from one horizon to the other. We were making for Bukama, a lonely place on the edge of a swamp with a bad reputation for fever. We had no difficulty finding it and the solitary hard gravel strip was better than we had expected, but what worried me was the fact that there was no shelter of any kind on the airfield. I dare not tell Barbara to take Alex into the shade of the jungle on either side of us for fear of snakes and ticks. They had no alternative other than to crouch under the wings in order to escape from the fierce heat of the morning sun. Just when I was debating to myself whether or not to take off in order to rouse someone from the village, I spotted a decrepit-looking lorry approaching from a tiny track I had noticed to our left. On board was the welcome sight of drums of petrol. After refuelling we wasted as little time as possible and, perspiring profusely, we all climbed into the Messenger and took off. Breathing freely once more, and sucking in the fresh air, we slowly gained height. As we continued our course towards Elisabethville the jungle now began to thin out and give way to dry hilly bush-type country. It was still intolerably hot and our rate of climb was poor and so bumpy that in spite of our safety straps we had to hang on to everything we could grasp. Alex thought it was great fun as his toys leapt up and struck the cabin roof, but Barbara hated every moment of it.

In time I was able to settle on course at 7,500 ft, persevering with the thermals and downdraughts with bored discomfort. I was otherwise thoroughly relaxed as we were out of the dangerous region and nearing civilisation. Suddenly a downdraught more severe than usual brought me out of my reverie; though I eased the nose up to maintain my height this was not sufficient and we continued sinking. I opened the throttle to the limit but it made no difference, and I soon realised that the machine was not running out of this particular downdraught into a compensating thermal as was usual under such circumstances; instead we were going down like a lift with the machine at full power and at its best climbing speed. Whereas a few moments earlier we had been looking down at the trees and hills way below us we were now too damned close for comfort. Ahead I saw one red craggy ridge sparsely covered with tinder dry bush grass, and realised we were not going to clear it. Without hesitation I turned the Messenger down the slope of the hillside with the throttle wide open and the machine at the best climbing speed. We held our breath in awful anticipation; then, as suddenly as we had begun, we now had to hang on as the aircraft shot up at an alarming rate. With the engine revs winding up I quickly snatched the throttle back to its normal position. Had I not acted as swiftly as I did I am sure we would have struck the hillside before we had run free of the downdraught. Barbara had sensed what was going on in my mind but had kept completely silent. Now she turned and smiled, placing a reassuring hand on Alex sitting in the back as she did so.

Shortly after this alarming incident we saw a huge column of smoke miles ahead but directly in our track. I knew it was a forest fire but as we had returned to our maximum cruising height I decided to hold my course. The Messenger bucked like a wild bronco in the hot disturbed air and the sight of the blazing inferno below was quite terrifying. Suddenly I heard a noise above that of the engine, and a startled Barbara heard it at the same time, so I momentarily closed the throttle, and in those few seconds we could hear the thunderous roar and crackle of the flames below as the fire tore across tinder-dry undergrowth with the speed and sound of an express train.

Elisabethville, with its wide tarmac runway and wooden customs and control offices, was a welcome sight. We had good friends in this established and well laid-out city, and our overnight stop was both comfortable and pleasant. In the morning I had a business call to make in the mining township of Nkana, where a flying club had shown interest in the Messenger.

The Northern Rhodesians, like their neighbours to the south, gave us a sincere and warm welcome. Although we had literally dropped out of the blue, they in no time at all organised a cocktail party enabling us to meet most of the Europeans in that part of the country. Many of these people had been away from their homeland for so long that they were aching for the latest news of conditions now that the war was over.

When, the next morning, I swung the Messenger's propeller, the engine was dead: the impulse magneto had broken. In quick time and without hesitation our new found friends insisted upon taking one from their old Tiger Moth and fitting it into our aircraft.

We were soon on our way to Ndola and Lusaka for our last night before introducing Barbara and Alex to their new home in Johannesburg. The following day I decided to fly via Bulawayo and Pietersburg in order to give Barbara and Alex an extra chance to stretch their legs before the excitement of the welcome awaiting us at Rand Airport. Pretoria gave advance notice that we were approaching a vastly different terrain from that to we had recently become accustomed. I was now able to point out in the distance the high-rise buildings, the slum-like sprawling native township and the ugly mounds of dusty sand from the nearby mines that gave this brutally vulgar place the original name of my Mew Gull – *The Golden City*.

*The grass airfield at Livingstone in Northern Rhodesia in May 1948. On the ground can be seen Tiger Moths and Avro Ansons. The author landed here on several occasions between 1946-8, flying Messengers, Geminis and a Dove.* (The Aeroplane photograph).

*Broken Hill, Rhodesia in May 1948. The airfield can be seen at top right.* (The Aeroplane photograph).

*August 1946 – the author and his son Alex en route for the Kruger National Game Reserve. TJ 1009, the author's grey short-chassis Packard Sedan, was the first to arrive in Johannesburg. (Author).*

*An aerial view of Johannesburg taken from Miles Messenger 2C G-AGUW by Ron Moulton during a flight with the author in March 1946.*

# Log of sales tour from Germiston June 10th–29th 1946 in Miles Messenger G-AGUW

| Date | From | To | Time | | Remarks |
|---|---|---|---|---|---|
| June 10 | Germiston | Bulawayo | 4 | 00 | |
| " | Bulawayo | Livingstone | 2 | 15 | |
| June 11 | Livingstone | Mongo | 2 | 07 | |
| " | Mongo | Vila Luso | 2 | 45 | |
| " | Vila Luza | Lobito | 4 | 20 | |
| June 12 | Lobito | Luanda | 2 | 35 | |
| " | Luanda | Local flying | | 45 | |
| June 13 | Luanda | Leopoldville | 3 | 25 | |
| June 15 | Leopoldville | Local flying | | 30 | |
| June 19 | Leopoldville | Moanda | 2 | 20 | |
| " | Moanda | Leopoldville | 2 | 20 | |
| June 20 | Leopoldville | Kolo | 1 | 00 | |
| " | Kolo | Leopoldville | 1 | 00 | |
| " | Kolo | Local flying | | 20 | |
| June 21 | Leopoldville | Moanda | 2 | 30 | |
| " | Moanda | Leopoldville | 2 | 00 | |
| June 22 | Leopoldville | Kitwit | 2 | 30 | Kitwit wrongly marked on map |
| " | Kitwit | Luluabourg | 2 | 50 | |
| June 23 | Luluabourg | Bukama | 4 | 00 | |
| " | Bukama | Elisabethville | 2 | 00 | |
| June 24 | Elisabethville | Local flying | | 30 | |
| June 25 | Elisabethville | Nkama | 1 | 05 | |
| " | Nkana | Local flying | | 30 | Impulse magneto failure |
| June 26 | Nkana | Local flying | | 25 | |
| " | Nkana | Broken Hill | | 55 | |
| " | Broken Hill | Lusaka | | 45 | |
| June 27 | Lusaka | Bulawayo | 4 | 10 | |
| June 29 | Bulawayo | Pietersburg | 3 | 10 | |
| " | Pietersburg | Germiston | 1 | 55 | |
| | | **Flying time** | **58 57** | | |

# CHAPTER 5

# DEATH IN THE DARK

Africa has always held a deep and compelling fascination for me. True, it could be cruel, harsh and relentlessly demanding but, at the same time, to those that accepted the terms of its vast equivocal and often mysterious terrain and obeyed its unwritten rules, it could also be kind, generous and endearing. It is a land one comes to love with an unimaginable intensity, as history has demonstrated in so many unexpected ways.

Africa was old and it was young – a paradox that only added to its subtle but magnetic attraction. We now lived in Johannesburg, the drama of history was more recent but nevertheless fascinating in that we were the onlookers as it unfolded before our eyes.

On July 10th 1946 I flew with Sir George Albu south to a little dorp by the name of Odendaals Rust where, at a public meeting, he was to oppose the establishment of a new township that was to be called Velcome. George said to me: "Alex, you are watching history in the making on the Transvaal, just as I did when my father first came to Johannesburg. This place, with its new gold seam, will become bigger than Johannesburg ever was." As I looked at the bare dusty scrub land of the surrounding high veldt, I could not believe this to be possible.

As the South African winter showed signs of the coming spring I was anxious to visit the Kruger National Game Reserve before parts of it were closed for the summer rains. Barbara and I set off on in high spirits in the car with Alex making excited comments from the back seat. Considering the rough dust-choking state of the main road all the way to the entry point into the game reserve at Pretoriuskop, our journey in the short-chassis Packard Sedan was made in luxurious comfort. The reserve was a wonderful experience for Alex. He loved animals and he was now able to observe otherwise dangerous species from the safety of the car, often at very close quarters. It was however quite tiring. All of us would be up at dawn, with Alex alert as a lark and eager to light the camp-fire, finish breakfast and start our first expedition. We would drive quietly and slowly along the tracks into the bush, peering intently and expectantly for signs of lion, buffalo or elephant. We were never disappointed but it was always three very weary and dusty travellers who drove into the night camp for a shower, drink and a hearty meal, followed by a wonderful night sleeping under a clear African sky.

The atmosphere on these occasions was so idyllic it seemed almost unreal. A camp-fire had usually been made by a young African before we arrived. On arrival we would start almost immediately our respective chores for the evening. Alex would collect stinkwood for the fire, Barbara prepared the evening meal and I would find somewhere suitable to sleep.

By the time we had all showered in the rather crude and austere ablution block and changed into something clean and comfortable, the sun would be sinking below the horizon, leaving shadows amidst the distant mountains. From the valley below would drift the sounds of wildlife, now aroused from long daylight slumber to slake their thirst on the banks of the slow silent ribbon of water that twisted its way in the distance. Before eating our evening meal we would sit beneath a *mapani* tree and sip our drinks in the fading light, watching the animals around us. Sometimes a steady cumbersome line of elephants would troop to a shallower and muddier spot of their choice, or buffalo would discreetly edge their way from the undergrowth a little further upstream. With the mountains silhouetted against the ever-changing burning sunset the valley came alive with noise. Every so often the flickering campfire spat a shower of sparks, combining to create an atmosphere that enthralled us all. No one spoke; our own silence was bliss.

After we had been at the Kruger Reserve three nights, travelling north all the while, I was anxious to show Barbara and Alex the last camp before reaching the Mozambique frontier marked on my map as Pafuri, where the winding river Limpopo flowed. We planned to rest overnight at Punda Maria but, because the area was in the process of being opened up as part of the National Park, no one seemed to know much about the facilities and accommodation. Unlike other camps such as Letaba and Shingwedzi, which had strong fences around their perimeters and small rondavels for sleeping, Punda Maria was merely a clearing in the jungle-like vegetation with a couple of small tents and a solitary African boy attending a well-stocked camp fire. When we arrived one tent was already occupied by a Dutch couple who appeared very relieved that they were to have company for the night. There were no shower facilities and as we had time to spare, and the sun had not yet reached the horizon, I suggested we might drive slowly along the banks of the Limpopo and watch the animals come out of the thickets on their way to water.

The track we followed in the twilight was narrow in the extreme and the vegetation pressed hard against the sides of the car. The air was hot, thick and humid and, as usual at that time of the evening, the place was coming to life. Against an incessant background noise of crickets, monkeys screamed their warnings from the trees and the odd firefly signalled that daylight was fast fading. As we moved silently and slowly the narrow winding track suddenly opened out into a glade, revealing a huge baobab tree in its centre. The sight before us stopped us in our tracks. Under this huge, gaunt and ugly tree were five leopards. As though hypnotised we watched them for a while, whispering to ourselves and utterly fascinated by the scene before us. As it grew darker I moved the car slowly closer. The leopards merely watched us and nonchalantly lolled against the tree trunk. As I moved closer still they casually rose to their feet and watched with bored unconcern as our grey car crept past.

In my anxiety to turn into the open glade for our return to the camp I inadvertently drove closer to the animals than intended. Immediately the slow somnolent attitude of the nearest leopard changed. Turning its head and twitching its tail angrily from side to side, it spat and hissed, then a front paw flashed out in a vicious sweep that missed the car by inches. They all then rose and sauntered casually off into the dark shadows and out of sight.

Our newly-found Dutch friends were disappointed when we related our experience but very happy that we had returned to keep them company during the night. After a meagre wash, refreshing drink and slow supper prepared almost by the light of the solitary camp fire, we retired to our tent and the Dutch couple repaired to their shooting-brake. Our quarters were very cramped. Barbara and I slept on a kapok mattress with Alex in his own sleeping bag between us.

We were almost asleep when the most blood-curdling roar rent the air from a few feet away. Barbara nearly leapt through the tent roof and I instinctively went for the automatic I kept under my pillow. Following the roar came deep heavy grunts as a lion tramped around the flickering fire. He uttered another roar and Barbara jumped out of bed. As Alex awakened I whispered sharply to Barbara: "Get back into bed and set an example to the child." Looking out of the tent I could see from the glow of the fire the whites of the lion's eyes. The African boy threw more wood onto the flickering embers and prodded them vigorously. From time to time he glanced apprehensively over his shoulder in the direction of the grunts as the lion slowly padded its way around the fringe of the small clearing. Prudence dictated that we should seek the security of the car, but I could not leave the African boy outside, unprotected and alone, and I decided otherwise. Barbara would certainly have not got into the car by herself, terrified as she was, so I felt we must stay where we were and remain alert. From time to time there were screams of warning from a baboon or a monkey, and a threshing in the undergrowth as something tore its way to safety. This situation continued for what seemed hours, sometimes so close that one could hear not only the deep grunt as the lion padded silently on the soft ground, but the hiss and escape of breath as the beast got more impatient for a kill. Suddenly there was a roar so thunderous and petrifying that we froze in our beds. Outside the tent there was the sound of scuffling bodies in furious entanglement as they tore through the undergrowth, dry branches snapping like matchsticks. Apart from the sound of other animals beating a frenzied retreat in the distance, there was comparative quiet. We listened in tense silence, until the danger appeared to have receded. It was only then that we relaxed and eventually dropped off to sleep.

On our return to Johannesburg I was pleased to hear that Miles Aircraft had completed the first export Messenger for us and that it would be delivered as far as Cairo. Our own demonstration machine, G-AGUW, could now be delivered to Albert Fischer in the Belgian Congo and it was decided that I should collect the new machine when ready.

By this time, as a family, we were beginning to get the feel of our new environment. We were sad and disappointed to realise that it was not the happy and tranquil atmosphere we had envisaged during those dull, dreary demanding days of war.

To us, Johannesburg was a harsh, brittle and glittering city filled with an even harder, less endearing cross-section of society than is usual. Most of us in England were in a state of shock immediately after the war and we looked forward, perhaps naively, to freedom, food, prosperity and sunshine. The thriving, bustling city of Johannesburg offered all these things and more, but it also had a darker, less glamorous and often cruel side. With the devastation and destruction of such a large part of Europe, and the persecution that prevailed in Germany during the prelude to hostilities, people from all walks of life had been attracted by the wonderful opportunities offered by this land of milk and honey – South Africa. Johannesburg attracted both the uppermost and the lowest of society, but I would not like to say in what proportions. At parties thrown by the likes of Sir George Albu or Errol Hay, father of Ian, it was possible to meet more royalty and peers of the realm than one would expect to come across in a decade of travel across Europe. In addition one would meet millionaires of the war years, as well as families of the pioneers of this land of opportunity: men such as Sir Alfred Beit, Sir Ernest Oppenheimer, Lord Robbins and Sir Abe Bailey, all of whom, endowed with a mixture of brain, brawn and determination that is common to many entrepreneurs, carved an empire where men of lesser calibre failed.

The darker side of society in Johannesburg at this time was the dregs of humanity who took advantage of the weaknesses and misfortunes of others, unscrupulously and devoid of any integrity or honesty whatever. Though agile and fertile of mind these people exploited every possible angle, and with a population clamouring for riches and quick profits their harvest, however tainted, was prolific. I met many of these hungry scavengers and at first it took me some time to pierce the façade of bogus respectability that their enormous wealth masked so convincingly. Fortunately I had some good friends who helped guide me through the many pitfalls set to trap the unwary.

And finally there was the ever-growing problem of black versus white. I have never been a racist but I am aware of the problems that can prevail. In South Africa the difficulties were immense and I could only listen, look and ponder upon the words of Jan Smuts, probably the finest statesman the Union ever had when he said: "This is a matter that only time will solve." How *much* time, I wondered.

A letter from the Woodley office of Miles Aircraft advised that our new

Messenger had left the UK en route for Cairo in the hands of a pilot named St. John. Not wasting any time Ian Hay took off for Leopoldville and I booked a passage on an Empire Flying Boat due to leave from Durban on September 7th 1946. Barbara and I were then young enough to enjoy crazy notions on the spur of the moment and when I suggested we should drive the 400 miles to Natal to enjoy a day on the beach before the flight, she accepted with alacrity. We drove through the cool of the night with Alex asleep on the back seat. We had a wonderful day dashing in and out of the warm sea with confidence, knowing that the heavy steel netting placed at suitable spots would protect us from the hungry marauding sharks.

The following morning I boarded the BOAC Short S.23 Empire Flying Boat G-AFBJ, with Capt. Whittaker at the controls. We had been in the air for about an hour when I heard the starboard inner Bristol Pegasus engine change note before suddenly emitting an unpleasant noise. In moments the engine was damped down and the pilot announced that we were returning to Durban. I rang for the steward and asked to speak to Capt. Whittaker. I asked him to radio base and try to locate my wife before she returned to Johannesburg. He willingly did so but after nearly an hour returned to say that they had been unable to trace her.

On landing back at Durban I remembered that Barbara had said she would take one last swim with Alex before setting out on the long hot return drive to Johannesburg. I borrowed a car with a driver from the BOAC manager and dashed off to the seafront looking for the number-plate TJ1009. With all the glittering vehicles crowding the promenade it was like looking for a needle in a haystack. I was about to give up when I let out a yell of delight as I spotted the low grey sports model almost where I expected it to be. In no time at all I surprised Alex as he was digging himself a sand castle on the beach. We were able to spend another glorious day on the beach together before I made a second attempt to reach our first destination *en route* for Cairo.

For sheer relaxed enjoyment I think travelling by flying boat over Africa in those days must have been the ultimate in flying. Though slow it was interesting and highly entertaining. The coastal scenery flying via Lourenco Marques, Beira, Lindy, Dar es Salaam and Mombasa was truly beautiful and restful to both mind and body. I have always been somewhat disenchanted with Kisumu but the gentle touchdown on the calm water, landing almost amidst the reeds and elephant grass at such places as Port Belle and Leropi, I found utterly fascinating.

We landed on the Nile in Cairo on schedule on September 11th after a little more than 36 hours flying time. I stepped into the launch with the smell of that hot sprawling city in my face and said goodbye to my friends of the past few days. Once ashore a noisy, excited and dirty Arab attendant hailed a dusty broken-down taxi at my request and we tore into the main stream of a seething mass of humanity. Some time later we pulled up at the imposing entrance to Shepherds Hotel. How we arrived there without accident I shall never know.

My plan was to locate the Miles Aircraft representative in Cairo in the hope he would have the Messenger ready and waiting for me so that I could quickly be on my way home. I was, however, in for a shock, for I could not find him, either in Cairo or at the aerodrome. I then telephoned the factory at Woodley, only to be told that the Messenger had left as arranged but would be including a sales tour of Yugoslavia and Greece en route. I was not at all happy with this. As a result of my call they instructed the pilot to proceed without delay.

Cairo immediately after the war was packed to capacity with civilians and service personnel trying to get out of the place to return to their own countries or to take up the offer of a wonderful life in countries such as Kenya, Uganda, the Rhodesias and the Union. Knowing that the Messenger did not carry radio I was aware that I might have trouble in passing through Khartoum and the Sudan on the flight back to Johannesburg, so I asked the Director of Civil Aviation if he could see his way clear to granting me a special dispensation to fly through this difficult sector without radio.

After he gave me the note of authority we went over to his club. As we sat down for a chat over our drinks a brigadier from a South African unit came over. After introductions were made he asked me if I would give him a lift to Johannesburg. As his bulk was enormous – he must have weighed at least twenty stones – I had great difficulty in containing myself as I envisaged the hilarious spectacle of this huge man trying to squeeze himself into my little aircraft. Smiling at him, I declined, giving the truthful excuse that I had not yet found the aircraft, and that I would in all probability be looking for a spare seat myself.

As the days and nights dragged on while I waited for the arrival of the Messenger I ground my teeth in rage at the uninformative manner in which Miles had arranged this collection. I could have kicked myself for my own stupidity in leaving Johannesburg before I knew the aircraft was at Cairo. I do not ever remember in my life being so frustrated. When I eventually traced the Miles representative, there was nothing he could do. I was constantly phoning Woodley but they were unable to contact the pilot of the Messenger. As a result I was compelled to squirm in silence as I suffered the hot, sticky, stinking heat of that overcrowded city, seeking refuge from time to time in the hotel dining room, the only part of the hotel that was air-conditioned.

One day, I was waiting my turn in the queue to use the hotel telephone when a swarthy, heavily-built man, perspiring profusely, stepped from the cubicle. He had such a forlorn look of utter despondency that I almost burst out laughing. As I did so our eyes met and he demanded: "What's so funny, what are you laughing at?"

Still laughing, I said: "I am willing to bet you a pound that you are in the same predicament as myself. You are stuck in this dump and you cannot get out."

"How did you know that?" he asked.

I told him that it was written all over his face. It transpired that he was a professor at the Tel Aviv University by the name of Wolfgang Yurgo and he was due that week to give an important lecture in Johannesburg, but was unable to obtain a seat on any aircraft. He was a very intelligent Jew and we spent a great deal of time talking of his life of persecution in Germany and his wartime experiences, most of which had been in Greece, Turkey and Egypt. Although German by birth he had been cruelly treated by the Nazis but had been fortunate enough to get out of Germany in 1938 and join the British Intelligence Service. He told of intrigue and plotting in Turkey and of the unscrupulous and sinister pressures that were exerted on one of Von Papen's senior female secretaries to extract information of the highest importance.

The other story he told was almost unbelievable. We were having our usual meal in the cool dining room one evening when Wolfgang pointed to a far table and said: "During a most critical phase of the war we executed a German officer over there." He went on to say that he was chief officer for the anti-Nazi German intelligence department and had formed a team comprising other British and American personnel. The practice, other than routine interrogation, was to pick out those Germans who might have information of value on the Nazis or had knowledge of our own plans and forces in the Middle East. From what he said I gathered that the grilling of certain prisoners was ruthless and extremely thorough and that each member of the team undertook a careful analysis of the results. For reasons that were not clear to me, it was decided on one occasion that a particular high-ranking officer possessed such a knowledge of both the Nazis' and the Allies' strategy and tactics in the Middle East zone that he was considered so dangerous he might jeopardise the progress of the war should he escape, or even be allowed to remain in captivity. After much deliberation a unanimous decision was reached – the man was too dangerous to live. On the pretext that the German officer was leaving for internment a sumptuous meal was arranged for him in company with an American and a British officer at Shepherds. After the Nazi officer had wined and dined extremely well a fatal dose was slipped into his glass and he collapsed over the table. Calmly, the head waiter was told to fetch a doctor waiting nearby. An ambulance was sent for and the body was removed quietly and without comment. Wolfgang went on to say that the British officer was curtly and coldly correct during the whole incident but, as much as he hated the Nazi officer, he could not forgive the American for slapping the prisoner on the back as he told him to finish his drink.

A few days later Wolfgang was lucky to get a seat on a crowded airliner. Giving him a letter to hand to Barbara on his arrival in Johannesburg, I said farewell. I now felt like a tiger in a cage. It was too hot to expend any energy and I occupied the time reading in the comparative cool of a pool under the palm trees, visiting an air-conditioned cinema or eating a long drawn-out lunch in the hotel dining room.

Visiting Thomas Cook's to find out what chance I had of obtaining a seat – should I need one – to Johannesburg I was dumbfounded to see not only crowds of people patiently waiting, but the enormous prices they were prepared to pay for a passage. I was so astonished that before I came away I had agreed provisionally to take with me three passengers should the Messenger turn up. Initially I wanted to settle for just two people with little luggage, but such was the urgency of the situation I was told to forget luggage and take as many people as I could get into the aircraft.

Out of the blue on the hot sultry afternoon of September 22nd a page-boy came to me with a cable saying that the wandering pilot with the Messenger would arrive that day. Invigorated, I rushed to inform my passengers and prepared for a dawn take-off.

*Rickshaws in a Johannesburg street in May 1948.* (The Aeroplane photograph).

*Short S.23 Empire Flying Boat G-AFBJ* Carpentaria *in which the author flew as a passenger from Durban to Cairo in September 1946. Completed in 1937 for Imperial Airways, G-AFBJ was delivered to QANTAS as VH-ABA early in 1938. In July 1942 the flying boat was restored to BOAC and finally scrapped at Hythe in 1947. During wartime service G-AFBJ was camouflaged and flew with blacked out windows. The red, white and blue stripes beneath the registration letters identify the 'boat as a civilian aircraft.*

# CHAPTER 6

# GREEK ODYSSEY

My spirits fell when Miles Messenger G-AHGE finally arrived at Cairo. The pilot casually announced: "The machine's OK but they didn't fit a mixture control when I left Woodley". I was not at all happy about this new problem. It was one thing to cross Europe without this mechanism but when I reached the high hot African shelf I knew I should need mixture adjustment. When I spoke to the Miles agent my spirits sank further – he did not have the spare parts and they would take time to make and fit. In my anxiety I foolishly decided to leave at dawn and deal with the matter at either Khartoum or Kisumu should it become a necessity.

I met my passengers for the first time under the poor light of the entrance of their shabby hotel. They were three Greeks by the name of Samaras, two brothers and a sister, none of whom spoke very good English. A dilapidated taxi rattled up and they began climbing aboard. I was staggered to see the amount of luggage they had brought and immediately protested in no uncertain manner. At first they refused to do anything. I thought they did not understand what I was saying so, speaking slowly and clearly, I told them that I would take only two of them with one case of luggage each. They understood this well enough and begged me to take them all, even if it meant leaving their luggage behind.

So we clattered off noisily and, with the roads now comparatively clear, made good time to Almaza aerodrome. From the shelter of the high buildings I was surprised and not a little concerned to see the winds gusting strongly and whirling sand into the air, to the discomfort of all.

Under the bright arc lamps on the concrete airport apron, on which the Messenger was gently rocking in the wind, I was able to take stock of my passengers in good light for the first time. Though they were all small in stature I was annoyed to see that they had tricked me over the amount of luggage they each carried. In the taxi they had surreptitiously stowed parcels under their legs. From one person I saw the top of a pot of home-made jam peeping from out of an old woollen jumper and from another I spotted the toe of a well-worn boot. I was now angry and I was about to tell them that I would take only two of them with me when I saw the look in the soft brown eyes of the woman. They were full of fear and she was close to tears. Her brothers meantime looked with apprehension at the small, fragile wooden machine as it rocked in the strengthening wind.

With a pang of conscience I realised what the ravages of war had done to these people. They looked at me fearfully, straining above the noise of the wind to catch every dreaded word I was about to say. I saw that they trusted me and each, in their own way, was trying to push thoughts of the imminent flight from their minds. Small and forlorn they may have been,

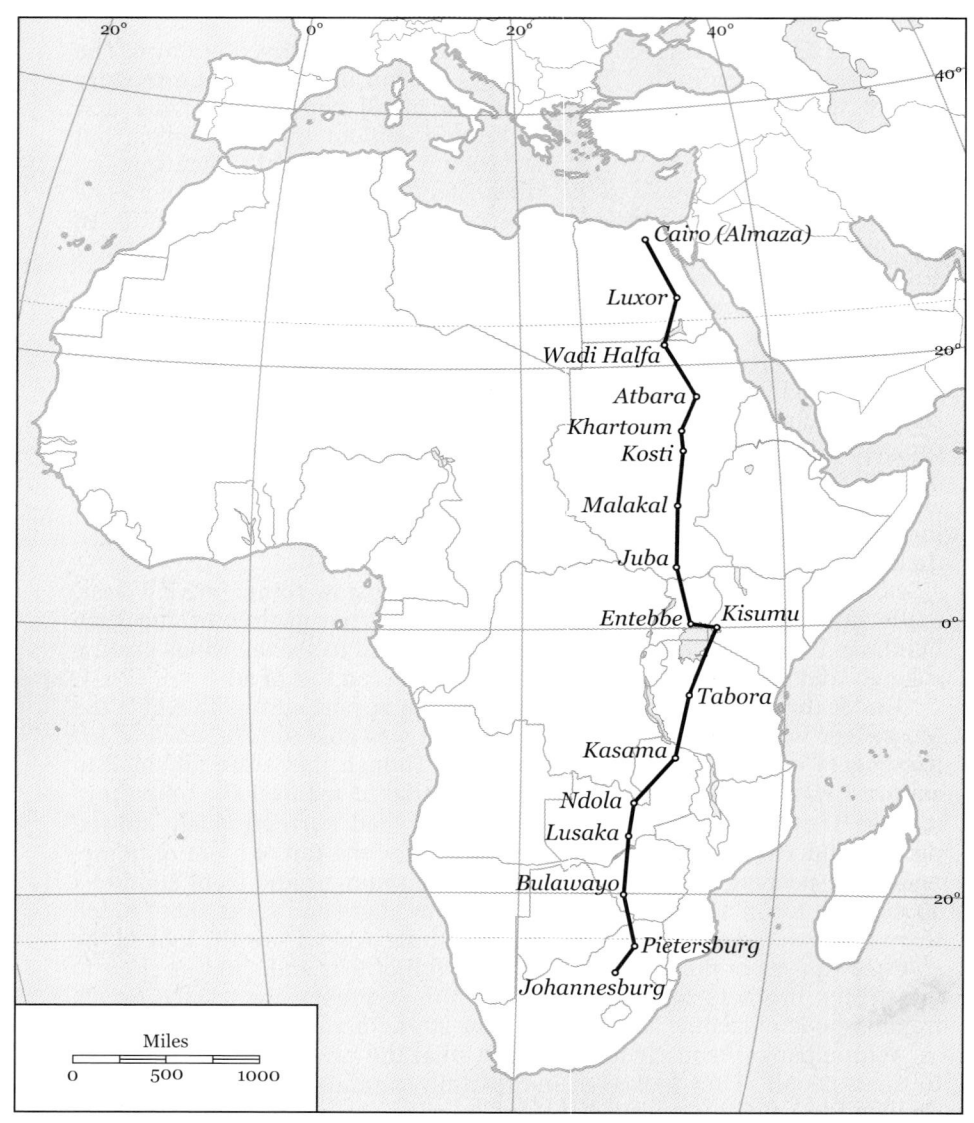

The author's route from Cairo to Johannesburg
flown in Miles Messenger G-AHGE in September 1946.

64

but they had guts. I am certain that had I asked the men to sit on the wings and the woman on the tail they would have done just that. I said, as gently as the wind would allow: "We have a long way to go and you are going to be very hot. You will be very cramped with all that luggage. We stop only at night for a meal." At this they looked as if they had been reprieved from a death sentence and smiles broke out for the first time.

My own problems now began. By the time we had loaded up and got to the end of the runway, dimly visible in the first streaks of dawn, the wind was rising to gale force; worst of all it was almost dead across the runway. The load I had on board put the centre of gravity of the Messenger on the aft limits and, as I opened up the throttle for take-off, I could not prevent the machine from weather-cocking and I was forced off the runway. I could also feel the crosswind flexing the stilt-like undercarriage and so I pulled up to a halt. On inspecting the ground at the side of the runway I was pleased to see firm sand, so I pointed the nose into wind and took off easily.

I climbed to find calmer air that would help my tense and cringing passengers to relax a little. The flying conditions were unpleasant for all of us, but with the River Nile now showing clearly below I had no navigational problems. In less than an hour the wind had abated and the air had become crystal clear. As we cut across the winding bends of the slow meandering river, the searing white heat from the hostile rocky terrain below could almost be felt as the heat from the rising sun reached its customary intensity.In a very short while I realised that even at this low altitude and in dry air, without mixture control I was burning far more fuel than I had anticipated. At this rate I did not have the four hours of duration necessary to reach Wadi Halfa and would now have to land at Luxor.

After landing at Luxor we refuelled quickly with barely a glance at the wonders of antiquity that small oasis had to offer. The Samaras took advantage of the welcome facilities whilst I checked the engine. With some dismay I discovered that the Gipsy was also using an excessive amount of oil. We were off the ground again in good time but it was not long before the clear air became diffused and overcast. My excessive drift warned me that the wind had returned once more. Arriving at Wadi Halfa the hot air and blinding sand made my task of refuelling difficult and unpleasant. Trying to taxi in the high wind, with the excessive load in the tail, controlling the aircraft was almost beyond me. Aware of my futile and often hair-raising efforts, the brother sitting at my side surprised me by putting his hand on my shoulder, saying he would climb out and assist by man-handling a wingtip. I must say I gave the little man full marks for guts – at times he was almost lost from sight in the whirling sand. When the wind gusted we were nearly airborne, with him clinging on for dear life. We managed to manoeuvre into a position from where I thought we could safely take off, but I dared not remain stationary as the Messenger was rocking badly and I could feel the wheels leaving the ground from time to time. Once more Samaras showed his calibre; as I kept the aircraft on the move he jumped onto the wing, literally fell into the cockpit and slammed the door. In a trice we were blown into the air and I struggled to keep the machine on an even keel.

To our intense relief, almost as suddenly as the storm had blown up, so it abated. Before us stretched the burning vastness of the Nubian Desert. By this time the heat and our exhaustive efforts had made us hot, dry, dirty and jaded, so much so that I was sorely tempted to do the unforgivable and fly direct across the desert to Khartoum. When I worked out my ground speed and checked the fuel once again I realised that, even if I flew a very accurate compass course, without a solitary fix, and hit Khartoum precisely, we would only just make it. The thought of the consequences of landing in that furnace below with three passengers, even though we might be within sight of the large city, made up my mind for me. We would instead fly the longer and safer route, round the Nile to Atbara.

By now the sun was way up and our dehydration rate so high that Miss Samaras was looking distinctly distressed. My own mouth felt as dry and brittle as parchment and my tongue rattled like a drumstick. Though my throat was not sore it was so dry I could not speak. The Samaras brothers seemed to be standing the rigours best of all, probably helped by the bottles of mineral water they had secreted amidst their numerous parcels. Though they had kindly offered to share their water with me I had noticed the sticky sickly-looking liquid and politely declined on the grounds of hygiene. I also did not wish them to suffer more discomfort as their stocks diminished as the day wore on.

Arriving over the small town of Atbara I circled quickly and landed on the desert that formed its airfield. Although I had travelled in these regions for many years I had never known heat so breathless and intense. We stepped out of the Messenger onto the burning sand as if into a fire. I hurried my passengers over to a small tin shed in the hope of finding water left for emergency purposes and to shelter them from the merciless sun. The corrugated iron door was fastened with a metal bolt but was not locked. I swung it open eagerly, and sure enough, there on the bare mud floor were two petrol tins with their tops crudely hacked off and half-filled with water. We rushed over to them and as I lifted one tin to my lips I saw inside a horrible mass of insect life and goodness knows what else. Despite this it took all my strength of will to refrain from filtering some of the precious liquid through my parched lips. I croaked at one of the Samaras brothers, who was not going to be put off by a few slugs, snails and algae, to put the tin down. He hesitated and would have ignored me, but I dashed the tin out of his hands and the slimy mass wriggled and crawled over his feet.

Any further argument was saved by the sound of an approaching lorry. It was with great relief that we saw an ancient vehicle swirling up the sand as it drove at break-neck speed with two forty-gallon drums of petrol swaying around in the back. The Egyptian driver was surprisingly alert and had left at the sound of my engine overhead. He had also anticipated our needs by bringing a case of drinks with him. Having first slaked our thirst the Samaras family crouched in the shade under the wings of the Messenger while I took the opportunity of cleaning the aircraft's large windscreen, which had collected oil, flies, and dust. As I rubbed the Perspex with a dry rag, the static crackled and sparked in an alarming manner. The shimmering vapour from the highly volatile fuel was rising from the aircraft in a mirage of waves; all it wanted was for a single spark to ignite that explosive mixture. Envisaging the inevitable explosion that would engulf us all I stopped immediately. We were quickly refuelled and I wasted no time in an effort to reach Khartoum before sunset. We landed there just after a Lockheed Constellation, having been in the air 11½ hours.

Khartoum has always conjured up a strange mixture of emotions and memories for me. That day it had the atmosphere of a once-busy desert aerodrome now partially abandoned with the aftermath of war. In equal portions it was occupied by the routine efficiency of BOAC, the authoritative flying control of the RAF and the lethargic and not very competent civilian customs and immigration control. The town was a mixture of wealth and poverty. It was sometimes sordid and depressing, yet in parts strangely dignified and quiet. The waters of the Blue Nile were quite beautiful. No matter how many times I visited this historic city the sickening heady smell of small operating theatres with neat, sparse, spotlessly clean wards came vividly to mind. In April 1938, during the survey flight preparatory to the Cape records, my father and I had a nightmare experience while flying the forbidden thousand miles direct-line route from Kisumu to Khartoum. Though we reached Khartoum by the skin of our teeth I arrived unconscious and was lucky to be rushed on a fire-tender to the finest hospital south of Cairo. It was an experience I was never likely to forget.

Once at Khartoum I now had other things on my mind. I first had to get my passengers settled for the night and then refuel the Messenger for a dawn take-off. Most important of all, I had to persuade flying control to allow me to proceed without radio across the sudd to Juba. Customs and immigration clearance presented no problems, but when I asked for food and drink I was told that there were no facilities. I pointed to the large American tourist group walking into a makeshift wooden reception centre and was informed that the American airlines had provided their own amenities until the civil authority could get re-established. As I had much to do I told the Samaras to follow me. We walked over to where the Americans were chatting excitedly as they moved slowly into the reception room, and nonchalantly joined in the party. With everyone talking to everyone else no one had a clue as to who we were. In no time at all we were offered sandwiches, coffee and cold drinks. Taking a quick gulp of lemonade I told the Samaras to find seats, as I was going to prepare the Messenger for our flight in the morning and would return to them as soon as possible.

Oil and petrol was no problem and, having checked the machine over carefully, I walked to flying control to deal with the last obstacle of the day. At first the RAF flying control officer was adamant. His instructions were that no aircraft was to proceed to Juba unescorted or without radio. When I showed him the special dispensation given to me by the DCA in Cairo he agreed, after some argument, that I could leave at first light in the morning. Later the Samaras and I crowded into one small taxi and drove into Khartoum to our hotel for the night. After a refreshing shower, a good meal and a final briefing with the Greeks I dropped into bed with the thought of the dreaded swamp between Malakal and Juba weighing heavily on my mind.

We got away so early the next morning that we arrived over Kosti, some 200 miles down the Nile, before the inhabitants of that small town seemed to be awake. Our low circuit must have stirred someone into life because we did not have long to wait at the grass airstrip before the usual petrol lorry trundled up to us.

At Malakal, further down the Nile, I was surprised on landing to receive VIP treatment from the RAF Station Commander, who said that Khartoum control had advised him of our departure. He had provided us with some tea and light refreshment in the protection of a small marquee. He was most kind and helpful but concerned that we were flying without an escort over the sudd to Juba.

In fact, on leaving Malakal, we had Juba in sight after about 3¾ hours' flying. My passengers seemed content and blissfully unaware of what was ahead of us. Only I knew what the enormous green swamp, glinting now and then with open water, contained. I could think of no worse place on earth on which to make a forced landing. On landing at Juba it appeared as abandoned as other airfields. A small RAF holding force willingly helped us get away in good time. With so many landings ahead of us I realised now that we would get no further than Kisumu that night; then at least the Messenger would have the protection of a large steel hangar, normally used to house the Short Empire Flying Boats, and there would be a small RAF contingent in charge of operations.

As I cleared for the early morning take-off I was astonished by the low calibre of the men. Their main occupation appeared to be ordering and kicking the local natives around orchestrated with a vocabulary consisting chiefly of four-letter words. I became so incensed by this needless display of arrogance and force that I told a corporal in charge that I wanted to see his Commanding Officer, only to be told that he was away shooting and would not be back for days.

At the crack of dawn the following morning, September 25th, we groped our way into the hangar, which was as black as night, and with the aid of a borrowed flash-lamp I pushed the Messenger out onto the tarmac apron. As my passengers were settling into their seats Miss Samaras let out a small cry and exclaimed that one of her small cases had gone. The RAF rating helping me said at once it was "the bloody natives." I was very angry: the case may not have been of much value but it meant a great deal to Miss Samaras, and I was morally responsible. The Greeks of course realised there was little I could do about it. Enquiries would achieve nothing and any small delay would mean another night away from their destination of Northern Rhodesia. What worried me more was that the machine was in a supposedly secure and locked hangar and, not having carried out an inspection of the aircraft, I did not know whether the aircraft had been tampered with, or damaged even. I was also cursing more than ever that I had been unable to rectify the mixture control back at Khartoum. Although the engine was running smoothly enough the consumption was reaching alarming proportions.

As I approached the deserted airfield of Tabora I flew only half a circuit, landed and taxied up to a half-hearted signal from an RAF rating near the control tower. I was now becoming accustomed to the postwar Service's desultory slaphappy approach, and here was no exception. In an oafish manner the RAF rating signalled me to stop. Bored and disinterested he then slouched off into the shade offered by the small control building. His hat was at a sloppy angle, his shirt was unbuttoned to the waist and his crumpled stockings had slipped to his ankles. As I helped the Samaras family down from the Messenger I heard behind me the sound of an authoritative step quickly descending the wooden staircase of the control tower. Without turning my head I saw from the expression on Miss Samaras' face that trouble was marching our way – from her demeanour it might have been the familiar tramp of the Nazi boot. As I turned I confronted a grim-faced RAF Flight Lieutenant, his hat set precisely square upon his head.

I realised at once that we must have appeared fair game for authority to flex its muscles. My passengers were not well-dressed, small in stature and almost cringing with subservience. My appearance was not much better. My normally smart and clean bush clothes were covered in oil and dirt and my topee, of which I was very fond, was now showing signs of more than a decade of wear.

"Are you the pilot of this aircraft?" barked the Flight Lieutenant. When I nodded assent he said: "I am the Commanding Officer of this aerodrome. You did not carry out the regulation left-hand circuit before landing and I have to tell you that I will not countenance any infringement whilst I am in control." Normally I would have just laughed at this, but his attitude in front of the Greeks triggered off my temper like a flash and I went for him.

"Don't talk like a bloody fool, we're in the middle of Africa, not Croydon. You have the registration of my aircraft, I will give you my name and I suggest you make out a full report and send it off, marked urgent, to the Director of Civil Aviation – it will give you something to do." I followed on, sharply: "It so happens that I am in a hurry and unless I get some fuel without any further stupid delays then I can assure you that *I* also shall have a report to make out when I reach Johannesburg." The Flight Lieutenant began to open his mouth, thought better of it and then shouted to the rating, who was now showing some interest in our presence, to get the oil and petrol over right away.

As I took off from the long runway I realised our troubles were not yet over. The high altitude of the landing grounds was now affecting the Messenger's performance. With the increase in temperature so the volumetric efficiency of the Gipsy engine would be further impaired. I got away from Tabora with no cause for alarm but it was still early in the day and the ambient temperature was comparatively low. I knew that I had one more vital full-load take-off to make before I reached the strip at Ndola where I would bid farewell to my Greek friends. The next landing, at Kasama, would also stretch my range to the limit and I had no alternatives to land at in-between. I knew that I had to hit this small strip in the bush right on the nose first time; any deviation and I knew we would have insufficient fuel to reach it.

The visibility was fantastic, though there was nothing to see but thousands of square miles of bush and yet more bush, and not a solitary fix to be seen. On the positive side I had an accurate compass course, a good watch and my trusty old slide-rule. Normally we would have been flying lower and wandering off track from time to time in pursuit of the enormous herds of wildlife, whereas now, after a slow laborious climb, I had levelled out at what I thought would give me the best height from which to spot Kasama. Our only company was a dust devil that whirled up from the hot arid plain below. I kept rigidly on course for hour after hour, checking the cloud shadow on the ground for the slightest change in wind direction. At the end of four hours I was sweating and on the edge of my seat. With the compass needle fixed determinedly on my calculated course, there were absolutely no signs of European settlement as far as the eye could see. My carefully worked out ETA gave me four hours and ten minutes to overhead Kasama, but I could still see nothing but bush. I reached for my slide-rule, calculated once more, and got the same result. Then, almost dead ahead, I saw a small group of buildings with a single airstrip alongside. Why I had not seen it from a distance I cannot say. As I pulled back the throttle our flying time was exactly four hours and ten minutes. I had watched my fuel gauges for so long as they reached the empty mark I was sure the engine would cut any minute.

I landed without hesitation and pulled up near an enormous European who waved to us cheerily with both hands. The moment I opened the cabin door I knew we were amongst friends. With a smile and a handshake he introduced himself and said: "I'll fill her up; you and your friends help yourselves to drinks and sandwiches in my office." When he asked me how much fuel to put in I told him how many gallons the port and starboard tanks held. When we all returned after a quick wash, with a cool drink and a sandwich in our hands, the refuelling had been completed. The aerodrome manager came up to me and said: "I think you must be wrong about those tanks, Alex, they took exactly what they should have done had they been empty."

I was not looking forward to the take-off. It was the hottest time of the day and previous experience with the Messenger told me exactly what to expect at this altitude and temperature with a full load. I said nothing however to my three sturdy little passengers. As I shook hands with the manager I told him that if I were not happy with the take-off conditions I would wait until the cool of the next morning. I taxied every foot of the runway before turning into wind for take-off. I made a mental note that if the Messenger were not airborne by the time we passed a certain *mapana* tree I would cut the throttle and wait for the morning.

I opened up and slowly we moved forward. Halfway down the strip we had gained sufficient speed to become airborne, but we were not flying, just riding along on that compressed cushion of air that had tricked me before. I was about to close the throttle and call it a day when a thermal caught the machine and suddenly we were 30 or 40 feet in the air. I thanked our good fortune and tried to gain a little more speed and reduce the angle of attack that was inducing so much drag. To my utter dismay the aircraft slowly settled back to within two or three feet of the runway. However, in my efforts to make use of the thermal, I had come to the end of the strip and to cut the motor now would mean disaster. Sweating profusely I hung on, hoping to God that there were no boulders or bushes in our flight path that would bring us down. As we carried on floating, as though on a large rubber ball, I eased the machine ever so gently to the right or left as each distant boulder or tree showed to be obstructing our path. The ground sloped slightly away to starboard and I hung on like grim death, coaxing the machine over the rough boulder-strewn grass, praying that I could keep from spreading us over the rocky ground, for with the tinder-dry grass we would have gone up in smoke on impact.

Slowly the aircraft began to respond to my coaxing and the gentle gradient. Gradually we gained a few extra miles per hour and then finally, after crossing another thermal that filled the cockpit with dust and leaves, I was able to ease down the nose slightly. It was only then that I felt able to slump back in my seat and take what seemed to be my first breath in hours. The Samaras, though aware of my tense anxiety, were of course oblivious as to its cause. Later, when feeling more relaxed I turned round to them and said: "You are nearly home now," they all smiled.

I dropped off my weary passengers at Ndola after passing them over to the Northern Rhodesian immigration officer. Knowing I was in a hurry to be on my way he said: "You get off, Skipper, I can sort this problem out for you." As I turned to say goodbye to my close companions of the last three days we were all embarrassed. Miss Samaras did not know whether to cry or kiss me. The look in the eyes of each brother was reward enough.

# Log of flight from Cairo to Germiston September 23rd–27th 1946 in Miles Messenger G-AHGE

| Date | From | To | Time | | Remarks |
|---|---|---|---|---|---|
| September 23 | Cairo | Luxor | 3 | 00 | With passengers |
| " | Luxor | Wadi Halfa | 2 | 45 | |
| " | Wadi Halfa | Atbara | 3 | 45 | |
| " | Atbara | Khartoum | 2 | 00 | |
| September 24 | Khartoum | Kosti | 2 | 00 | |
| " | Kosti | Malakal | 2 | 45 | |
| " | Malakal | Juba | 3 | 30 | |
| September 25 | Juba | Entebbe | 3 | 50 | |
| " | Entebbe | Kisumu | 1 | 50 | |
| September 26 | Kisumu | Tabora | 3 | 40 | |
| " | Tabora | Kasama | 4 | 10 | |
| " | Kasama | Ndola | 2 | 50 | Dropped passengers |
| " | Ndola | Lusaka | 1 | 55 | |
| September 27 | Lusaka | Bulawayo | 3 | 45 | |
| " | Bulawayo | Pietersburg | 2 | 50 | |
| " | Pietersburg | Germiston | 2 | 10 | |
| " | | **Total time** | **46** | **45** | |

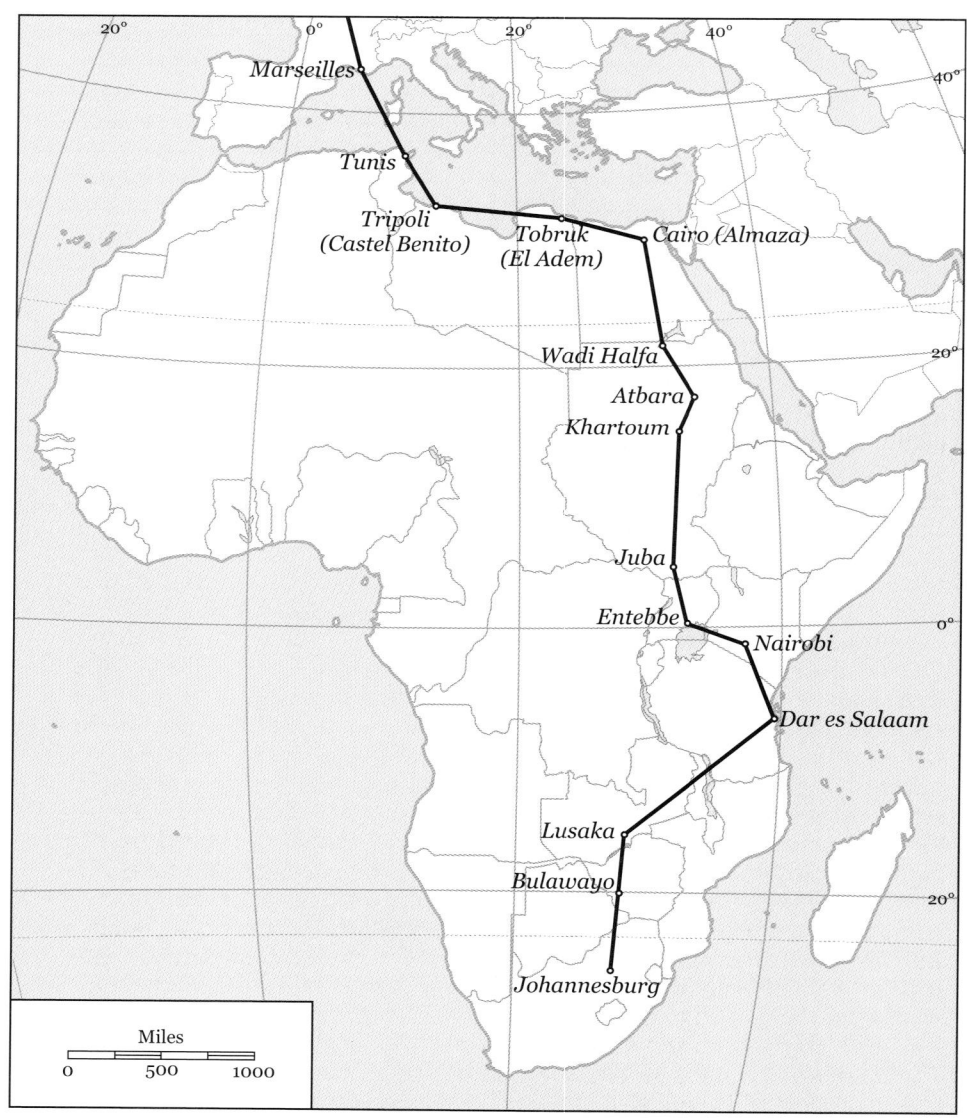

The author's route from Lympne to Johannesburg,
flown in Miles Gemini G-AISD in April 1947.

# CHAPTER 7

# "WHAT THE HELL DOES HE WANT TWO ENGINES FOR?"

The excitement and delight of my return to Barbara and Alex, after the vexations and frustrating absence of nearly three weeks in Cairo, was tempered somewhat by what I was told concerning their own experiences. The little bungalow and the environment in which we now lived on the outskirts of the city did little to endear us to Johannesburg, or lift our morale. Every time I thought about it my spirits sank and I realised that we must make up our minds about whether or not we should return to England.

In some ways the situation in which we were now placed was due to my own procrastination. Since taking up my appointment Robbie and Ian had done all they could to help me settle in and become established. Robbie had driven me to the outskirts of Johannesburg and introduced me to a friend who was then considering the sale of his delightful property. It would have suited us admirably but it was very expensive and not available on lease with an option to purchase. I knew that if I did not accept the offer there and then the property would be placed on the open market and be snapped up on the first notice of sale. At the time Barbara had not arrived and it was not a decision I cared to take on my own, probably because even at that early date I felt that she was not going to like living in South Africa.

I would then be left to find furnished accommodation, the most difficult type of residence to acquire during those early postwar years. There were thousands of refugees from Europe, servicemen being demobilised by the trainload, to say nothing of local civilians clamouring for the good life in this dazzling city. I had the good fortune to meet the owner just before he put the property in the hands of the estate agents. We got on well at first sight and he told me I could have the property if I went at once to his agent. The manager of the estate office already had several clients lined up for such a "desirable" residence and it was only when I insisted that he get in touch with the owner that he gave way and prepared a lease for me.

It was not a happy bright home that I was preparing for my little family. But for the wonderful kindness and hospitality of the Albu family, who insisted I should stay with them during those early months, I am not sure I would have remained to allow Barbara to confirm what I already felt.

Our black African servants lived in small rondavels built in the garden. The European owner had told me that he never employed male staff but only experienced Zulu girls. The local grapevine worked so rapidly that I had only been away from our new house for a few days when Lena, our warm, loveable and ever-smiling Zulu, came into the living room to tell Barbara that a man at the back door wished to speak to her. Puzzled,

Barbara went through the kitchen and discovered a rough-looking local who asked if he could use the telephone, explaining that he used to work for the old boss who owned the house before we came. My wife, knowing what I had told her, asked the man to wait for a moment. She rushed into our bedroom and from a hiding place grabbed my automatic. She then returned to the back door and as she opened it she clicked a bullet into the gun's breach and said: "The old boss never employed boys, so you are lying. You see this gun, if I ever see you on my property again I'll put a bullet through you." The man did not wait to hear any more but bolted; in the background Lena was convulsing with laughter.

On another occasion Barbara was disturbed by a rumpus in the road outside. She switched off all the lights and peered through the curtains. In the dim moonlight she saw figures turning off the road into our own drive and crouch behind the shrubs. Almost immediately armed police appeared, shouting orders. Suddenly there was a burst of machine-gun fire followed by screaming and the blare of sirens. Ambulances soon arrived amidst much noise and more sirens. Bodies were then picked up by the police and thrown into the ambulance, and silence prevailed once more.

Another night Barbara heard a scratching at the window. In response to her query one of the other native girl servants who lived in the other rondavel whispered in a terrified tone that Lena was groaning "something terrible" and would "missus" come at once? Barbara knew that Lena was pregnant and that for the other girl to venture out in the middle of the night on her own she must be very ill. Without hesitating Barbara checked the gun's safety catch, opened the door and went over to Lena's room twenty or so yards in the garden. As she opened the door she was confronted by a huge bare bottom, well up and fully exposed to view, with a newly-born piccaninny as black as the ace of spades curled up on the bare floor. There was Lena on her hands and knees, the whites of her eyes enormous as she looked over her shoulder with relief at Barbara's arrival.

While I was away in Cairo, in one week there were more than two hundred cases of rape, assault, robbery and murder in just one area of Johannesburg alone. It reached the point where we never got out of the car in the dark, even to open the garage door, without a gun. When driving in some of the suburbs we never halted at traffic lights and even in daylight, when stopped at a red light in the city, we made sure the passenger door was locked. There had been too many cases when an innocent driver, travelling on his own in a busy street, was suddenly aware at traffic lights that he had a passenger and there was a gun poked in his ribs. The driver would be told to drive into the country, where he would be robbed and beaten up, and his car driven away by a jubilant gang.

I had always looked upon the different African races in rather the same manner in which I later studied American Red Indian tribes. I was interested and intrigued by the differences in their customs, characteristics and the environment in which they established their nation, and ultimately their change and reaction to intervention by the white man. In my mind's eye I could picture the tall men of the Watusi tribe in the Ruwenzori mountains, the proud and disdainful Masai in Kenya, the good-looking women of the Hereros in South West Africa and of course the warrior-like tribes of the Zulu nation in Natal. I met dozens of other nationalities during my travels up and down Africa but I had neither the time nor the ability to study and examine their history and origins as I would have liked. My favourites, above all other tribes, were the Zulus. These proud, jovial people with their wide endearing smiles and rollicking sense of humour, coupled with their often enormous bulk, and who showed terrifyingly courageous behaviour in battle, attracted my curiosity. As servants they were often like mischievous children; indolent, noisy and sometimes naughty. But they proved their loyalty to us on more than one occasion, particularly where Alex was concerned. Like children they were attracted to glittering trivia and could be cunning in their acquisitiveness. Those in the Albu staff were from another tribe and were well-trained and, dressed in their immaculate uniforms, dignified, well-behaved and conscious of the position they held in the family. Our Zulu servants were younger and less responsible, but so much part of the household that when we parted the loss was deep and sincere. Not all Europeans would reflect our point of view and I must say that with the raging crime rate amidst the blacks they may have had some justification.

The first person to whom I sold an aircraft in South Africa was Charles Taylor, a diminutive but dynamic man with bright, sparkling, intelligent eyes. He had built up a successful engineering business in Johannesburg and had branched out in farming in Natal, where he had property on the River Tugela and another high up in the Drakenburg Mountains. We got on well together and I enjoyed immensely our trips together out into the country. Once, I took an unusual route to his farm that led us into the very heart of Zulu territory. We left the hard, corrugated road near Vreda and were soon driving slowly due east over grassy cattle tracks sometimes obstructed by huge boulders. As we cautiously travelled up and down these rolling hills, with the faint trail and the sun our only guide, we suddenly found ourselves amidst native mud *kraals*. They were neat and clean with hundreds of families busily engaged in their household duties. At our approach the children gave up playing and chasing the cattle and ran forward. The mothers paused over their fires but the head of the family merely raised his head from the comfortable seat in the sun outside the *kraal*. The oldest wife, distinguishable by her headdress, spoke sharply and the younger wives carried on with their work. There was a time when the glint of a steel assegai would have shown, but those times had long since passed. It was not difficult though to build up a picture in one's mind of these enormous men in battle. Their strength and courage was legendary and but for the rifle and the Gatling gun the British and the Boers would have taken a much longer time in dominating the beautiful country over which we now drove.

Charles Taylor had bought the Messenger as a safe and comparatively quick means of travelling to and from his Natal farms. His son John, who had just taken his licence, was to fly the machine. As I have said, one farm was at sea level and situated on the historic River Tulega; the other was located high in the Drakensburg Mountains. My first approach to the latter was in a Jeep. As we reached the summit after a breathtaking crawl along a precipitous gravel track hanging on the mountainside, I was surprised to lurch suddenly on to the small but level grass plateau that was to serve as the airstrip. I soon told Charles that having a strip at such altitude would present few problems for landing but warned that taking off might be another matter. The Tulega landing strip was however typical of that part of the world.

I delivered Charles' Messenger G-AHGE from Germiston to Tulega on October 25th 1946. After making a number of fully loaded take-offs and landings in the heat of the day, I found the approaches and the strip itself adequate for such a machine. The day was however marred by near tragedy. John Taylor, with all the brash confidence of youth, insisted on flying from the strip on his own. Instead of first carrying out a normal circuit and landing he flew straight off to visit neighbours in the area. On the return flight he decided to fly very low over the water, following the bends of the River Tugela. At a certain point, not far from where we stood, a steel cable had been strung across the river to transport logs and building materials. Travelling at maximum speed the Messenger struck this cable exactly in the centre of the propeller boss, stretched the cable like a giant catapult until it snapped, and crashed into the water. The impact broke up the wings and fuselage as if the machine had been a plywood tea-chest. Thrown clear, fortunately without being knocked unconscious to drown, Taylor hung on to the tangled remains of the aircraft in the fast-flowing river, fortuitously anchored by the wire cable, rather like a wooden float on a fishing line. By this time young Zulus were running and shouting all over the place and it was not long before John was dragged ashore looking very much the worse for wear, very frightened and not a little contrite. The outcome to that little incident could be summed up as follows: John had learnt a good lesson, I was able to sell another Messenger and the insurance company put up their premiums on the next machine!

Next day, I was late arriving at my office in the General Mining building. I shared a large room with Albert Robinson and Ian Hay, but both were absent: Robbie, as a Member of Parliament, was attending a meeting, and Ian was ill with malaria. Mrs Signe Worthington, our very competent secretary, heard me arrive and hurried over to say that Sir George Albu wanted to see me right away. With a whispered note of caution she remarked: "He has an odd-looking man with him."

Whatever might be said of our business activities in the General Mining Building, and however one might proclaim dislike of some associations, we were never bored. As the main South African office for the General Mining & Finance Corporation, it was built in the days when gold mining was its only source of revenue. With the end of the war in Europe the Company Chairman, Sir George Albu, was eager to diversify the company's commercial enterprises. Apart from the main business of mining, we on the periphery found ourselves involved in textile production, the import and export of a wide range of goods, breweries, aircraft charter, sales and service and, of course, George and Robbie's political and charitable activities. People constantly visited our offices from all walks of life. It was not uncommon, for example, to have royalty from Yugoslavia making social overtures in one part of the building, while in another room some crook could be expanding with wild enthusiasm his scheme for making money.

As I opened the door to Sir George's office I took in the situation at a glance. I saw a well-built, hard, tough-looking man with 'London underworld' written all over his face. Next to him was a woman in her thirties who matched up to her rough-looking companion. As Sir George introduced us I was somewhat startled to hear the woman say that she already knew me. When she repeated her name it all came back to me. When I terminated my job as chief test pilot at Vickers-Armstrongs I had sold the last of my three Hawker Tomtits to Messrs Shackleton, the aircraft sales company. They in turn had sold one of them on to the Dutch woman that now stood before me. Apparently she had just flown from England with a Miles Aerovan while her companion, whose surname was Bruce, escorted her in another. Having flown as far as Rhodesia the pair wanted to bring the machines on to Johannesburg. Eyeing Sir George, and knowing that he had a very full programme that morning, I suggested to our visitors that we should continue the discussion in my office.

The conversation that followed was much as I expected. I nevertheless took down all the details and promised to advise them as to the best way to proceed by the next afternoon. As he was about to leave, Bruce put his elbows on my desk and in a low, conspiratorial voice announced that he wanted to get into the diamond racket. As I knew my way around, he said, he would make it worth my while if I could put him in contact with the right people. I told him that we did not deal in diamonds but I could telephone a friend who would be happy to show him a very wide range from which to choose. Bruce laughed and with a smirk said: "I can get those bloody stones at home, I mean the ones they don't know about."

I said: "Do you mean illicit diamond buying?"

He said: "I don't know what *you* call it but I can tell you this, I haven't come all this way to pay through the nose for some polished bits of glass."

Keeping my temper under control I stood up and said: "Now, Bruce, you listen to a few words of advice. In the first place you have come to the wrong office for what you are searching and, secondly, if you do find what you are looking for I should be very careful what you do. You may think you can take care of yourself but there are some very rough boys out here and they may not take kindly to outsiders muscling in."

As Signe Worthington showed the pair out I got on the telephone to London and during a two-minute conversation my first feelings about Mr Bruce were confirmed. Weeks later, my meeting with Bruce and his Dutch lady friend forgotten, I happened to pick up a copy of the *Star* newspaper and there, right in the centre of the front page, was a very good head and shoulders photograph of Bruce. He had certainly found his illicit buying group, only they had welcomed him by shooting him dead at close range. They then dumped his body in a forty-gallon oil drum, saturated it with petrol and burned the remains to a cinder. The South African police did a good job solving the murder; through a painstakingly diligent search, with the help of the British police and dental surgeries, his molars identified Bruce's charred remnants.

In spite of our own misgivings, there is no doubt that the way of life in this scenic land of sunshine and blue skies was, after the hardship of war, idyllic. My work, though not demanding, was interesting and gave me all the opportunity to travel I could wish for. Our weekends were the happiest times. We would either motor over to George and Betty Albu's farm north of Pretoria, where we could ride, shoot, swim or just relax, or we could make sorties to various places of interest within a weekend range of car travel. Holiday leave was also generous and in January 1947 we spent a month casually motoring down to Cape Town via Kimberley and the Karoo, returning by the well known 'garden' route. There, Alex was able to enjoy the clean golden beaches and the exciting tussle as he dived fearlessly into the turbulent, pounding waves as Barbara and I watched. If anyone had asked us at that moment why we wanted to return to a drab life in England, neither Barbara nor I could have given a logical reason. But the fact remained, we pined for our homeland.

With the increase in our business commitments, and the news that Miles was nearing completion of our first twin-engined Gemini, it was decided that I should visit the UK and return with the new aircraft. The journey back would enable me to test the Gemini thoroughly in tropical conditions. I said to Barbara that the visit home would also give me the opportunity to find out what living in England was like during one of the hardest winters for many years.

I left Johannesburg for England on February 13th 1947 in South African Airways DC-4 Skymaster ZS-AUB. The flight was made all the more enjoyable when Captain Williams invited me to fly that four-engined flagship of the postwar airline. After 26 hours' flying we arrived over Heathrow the following day, having stopped over at Malta. As we broke cloud and descended in the gloom to land at Heathrow, the sight and atmosphere was depressing beyond measure. Although it was still early afternoon, after the brilliant sunshine to which I had become accustomed it seemed to me like night, and I could not understand why the lights were not switched on. With Heathrow in a state of development contractors' machinery, materials and rubble were strewn all over a sea of mud. The mud had been trampled into the assembly of dirty wooden sheds that served as temporary offices and clearance for customs and immigration. The raw, cold and damp air penetrated my clothes in spite of the fact that I had come prepared wearing woollen underwear and a heavy overcoat. As I fumbled for my passport I complained about the poor light and the immigration officer, with typical British phlegm, admitted that it had been somewhat difficult since the fuel crisis.

The warmth of the welcome awaiting me at Woodley certainly made up for the cold of the winter. Enthusiasm always prevailed at the Miles factory especially when in discussion with Blossom, Fred and George Miles and with such old friends as Tommy Rose, 'Bush' Bandidt, Ken Waller and Air Commodore Rowley. I realised just how much I had missed the camaraderie of flyers I had known for so long. Be it peace or war, we all sparked on the same wavelength. It was good to feel the spirit that enveloped the entire factory, in spite of the depressive socialist postwar restrictions of rationing, fuel cuts, and the worst winter in living memory.

My Gemini was far from completed and it was not long before I learnt of some of the difficulties facing the workforce. No matter how talented, adept and buoyed up by the tremendous potential that the future offered, it faced a growing bureaucracy that appeared to take great delight in being obstructive, with one obstacle following another. In the end even the most ardent believer in Britain's future began to get disheartened. During the war I had maintained that 'impossible' was a word that did not exist in the English language. The postwar England that I had returned to, with its hundreds of forms to be filled in triplicate, and more, told me otherwise.

I had many appointments with companies in and around London and, equipped with a small car and a bundle of petrol coupons, I set out determinedly to make the best of everything until the Gemini was ready to be test-flown. It was a depressing experience. Even so the indomitable good-humoured British made light of electricity and fuel cuts and the other hardships of the bitter weather.

Many of my calls took me to large modern offices. They were unforgettable sights: chilly unheated rooms, secretaries and executives wrapped up in overcoats and scarves; typists, often wearing fingerless gloves and peering over their keyboards with a candle stuck on the typewriter. Food of course was rationed and after the bountiful tables of South Africa I found the fare offered at most hotels and restaurants meagre, dull and unappetising.

As George Miles had offered me the use of any aircraft they had in service, I was free to fly at will. On March 10th I climbed into Miles M.18 G-AHKY and headed north from Woodley over the frozen countryside to visit my father in Lincolnshire. Unfortunately all the ground near my own landing field was so deep in snow that I dared not risk using it. The only runways cleared of snow at that time were at RAF Coningsby some 30 miles from where my father lived, and after a flight of 1 hour 45 minutes I landed there. The conditions were so bad that my father made three attempts by car to reach the aerodrome and succeeded only after leaving two cars deeply imbedded in snowdrifts at the side of the road.

I tried to persuade my father to fly back with me to Johannesburg but he declined owing to the pressure of work. A large organisation almost erased by the war needed re-establishing and what with the new bureaucracy and difficulties, plus the frustration endemic in such a rigidly controlled system, the prospect of success was made less promising and more arduous than necessary. He did however agree to fly out to us later in the year.

When I flew back to Woodley on April 1st work was completed on the Gemini and I was able to make the first test flight of G-AISD on April 3rd. With all the documentation cleared after much argument, I was able to leave for Africa that afternoon.

A slow cold thaw had set in during the past week or so and had produced the most appalling weather, with grey wet cloud hanging in the treetops. I had promised my father that I would fly up and say goodbye before leaving the country. As if sensing my wishes the cloud lifted, the sky was blue and I set off.

The sunshine glittered on the wet fields below as I impatiently set off for Lincolnshire, working out in my mind that I could return south and land at Lympne on the Kent coast provided I did not spend too much time with my father. However, when I circled my father's home I saw much of the grass under water. I decided to use the closed airfield at RAF Strubby, which had tarmac runways and was so well known to me during the war. This all took more time than I had anticipated and by the time I had said farewell to my father I knew that I would be landing at Lympne in the dark. I was not unduly worried and although I was sure that Lympne did not have landing lights I knew it well and, in such clear conditions, it raised no problems.

I set a very accurate course across the Wash and struck my first fix right on track. As I bent over to pick up my next map for the area further south I could not find it, even after a thorough search. The weather was good and the Gemini was purring along so well. Contented with thoughts of returning to Barbara and Alex I was confident that when I struck the south coast, even if a little off track, I could find Lympne. The light was now fading and as I crossed some of the higher ground over Suffolk I was surprised to encounter some banks of broken cloud. I assumed it was the aftermath of the bad weather we had recently experienced and as I expected to strike the coast in a few minutes there was really nothing to be concerned about. It was not long before I could see a faint coastline ahead with the dull glow from a light here and there. The dark flat carpet below was, I assumed, one of the numerous Essex marshes. Soon I was flying over water and could just see the dull outlines of various craft weathercocking with the tide.

I was just making up my mind that I would be foolish to try and reach Lympne in such conditions, and should make for Ramsgate or Gravesend instead, when I passed a large ship at anchor. I was suddenly conscious that her masthead navigation lights were too damned close for comfort and I realised that the cloud was forcing me ever lower. To cap it all it was raining hard and even with the port side-window fully open I could see less and less. Although I knew where I was, without a map the chances of locating Ramsgate or Gravesend were slim. I then remembered that very high-tension cables crossed the Thames and that their tops would not only be in cloud but their bases would be unseen in the dark. I could fly back on a reciprocal course on instruments to Lincolnshire and land on the beach but this weather front was getting worse by the minute and could already have covered the area I had just left. I could have wept with remorse. I had made the stupid kind of mistake one would expect of a pupil; in my impatience to return to my family I had ruined everything. If I was going to save my skin I had to act without further delay. I would have to make a crash-landing. If I got away with it the aircraft would take months to repair, if indeed it would be repairable. I felt dry in the mouth and sick in the stomach but the sudden swerve to avoid an unseen ship's mast brought home to me in no uncertain manner that I had to do something, and quickly.

I swung the Gemini due west and in minutes the darkness below me gave way to the dull lights of a village or a town. I guessed that the solitary lights would be an isolated farm on the fertile marshland. I strained my eyes peering through the small side window, my face cold and wet from the steady downpour. I saw the dim outline of a large building upon which was fixed a single light. The surrounding ground could have been anything but as I switched on the landing light I caught a glimpse of what appeared to be a large hedge. Using the light on the building to orientate my position I throttled back both engines, put down the flaps and criss-crossed as slowly as I dared towards the dark patch which appeared to run parallel to the hedge on which I was concentrating my search. It looked to be level and I assumed it was a ploughed field with the thorn-like hedge forming its southern boundary. I muttered a small prayer to myself and set the machine into wind for the final act of this sorry incident. I came in from the west with the light on the building now on my starboard side. I set the Gemini in a position of high angle of attack and put on plenty of power with the intention of landing alongside the hedge after passing over the buildings. The beam of the landing light showed the rain pouring relentlessly, but in my anxiety I was completely oblivious to the cold and the fact that my neck and shoulder were saturated by the water running down my face from the open window. As I was about to ease back the throttles the beam cut across some tall trees. I gave a burst of throttle on the engines to avoid them and had a quick glimpse of a small shed and what I thought to be a gate. Guessing it was the farmyard adjoining a field I eased back the throttles once again and as the landing light illuminated the glistening wet arable I switched off the engines. As the wheels touched ground I held the stick hard back into my stomach. Feeling as though it was sliding rather than running along the ground the aircraft quickly came to a standstill. I felt the wheels dig into the thick mud and as the tail rose from the ground I braced myself for the crunch. Luckily, at that moment the Gemini's wheels moved a little in the greasy wet slime and the aircraft stayed poised, as if on a tightrope, before falling back heavily to bury its tail wheel well and truly into the Essex clay.

I switched off the landing beam and sank back in my seat with relief. I had got down safely, thanks to God, but there was little excuse for rejoicing. I realised at once that I would not be able take-off from the surrounding quagmire and the task of moving the machine to a suitable grass field would be a long and difficult one. As I sat mulling over the ridiculous situation into which I had got myself I heard a shout. Opening the cabin door I saw the farmer, whose field it was, peering at me with the aid of a hurricane lamp. When I told him of my plight he said: "Good job you landed in me biggest field, it's ten acres and we haven't sown it long. Come and have a bite to eat and we'll see what we can do in the morning."

I had a simple but pleasant meal with a homely, friendly farming family and afterwards they took me to a comfortable little room. I was just getting into bed when I heard a loud hammering on an outside door. The farmer called to me that the police were at the door and wanted to see me. I went down, to be confronted by a constable, a sergeant and an inspector, all with expectant looks on their faces. I showed them my passport, explained what had happened and gave them names of reputable people that they might telephone to confirm my identity. The constable and sergeant were obviously quickly satisfied but the inspector was of a different type; he did not believe my story, would not telephone any of the people I had put forward and finally demanded to search the machine. I took the aircraft keys from my pocket and handed them to the inspector.

Coldly, I said: "If you think I am coming out with you in this weather you are very much mistaken. Here are the keys, search the machine yourself. I am very tired and I am going to get some sleep." With that I asked the kindly farmer if he would ensure that I had my keys returned that night. As I strode off to my bedroom I turned to the inspector and told him I would hold him personally responsible for any damage to the machine. As I snuggled despondently into my bed I pondered on what faced me in the morning, before dropping off to sleep dimly conscious that the wind and rain were beating on my window with increasing intensity.

I was so tired that I slept soundly and it was first light before I awoke to the sound of a howling and buffeting as a gale-force wind lashed the bedroom windows. Normally I should have been very concerned for the safety of the Gemini but as I awoke the enormity of the task ahead took all other thoughts from my mind. Damage to the machine by the gale seemed much the least of many other evils. As I looked dejectedly out of the windows I suddenly became attentive. I noticed that the wind was due east, which I remembered was the direction I had landed in the night. The gale, I reasoned, might be a blessing in disguise. My new-found friends insisted I had a good breakfast and after I had paid my hosts, after many protestations, and thanked them for their kindness, we pushed out into the shrieking wind. In daylight we walked across the farmyard and there in an adjoining field was the Gemini, firmly stuck and rocking every time a particularly strong gust threatened to tear it away from the sticky mud in which it was bedded. About two hundred yards ahead was a smaller hedge than the one that ran adjacent to the south side, and for the first time, I realised how lucky I had been. The farmer had just offered to fetch his tractor when two men turned up. I said that if I could warm up the engines, with one man under each wingtip with another rocking the tail, the machine might lift itself out in such wind.

Even before I climbed aboard the Gemini was shaking as the wind tore at it. Fortunately it was facing straight into wind and if I could only get the wheels out of the mud she would be almost airborne. The engines started immediately and after a sharp warm-up I signalled to my helpers that I was ready to open up to full power. As I did so nothing budged; the aircraft was fixed solid as though it had been tied down. After a short discussion I decided on another attempt, this time telling the man on the tail to push hard to one side and then pull it back as the men on the wingtips helped him in the same direction. I warned them to take care if the machine suddenly lurched forwards. Again I opened the throttles to full power and again nothing happened. I signalled desperately to the men on the wings to rock them. Suddenly there was slight movement to port and then, as the men rocked the aircraft the opposite way, everything happened at once. The Gemini gave a sudden lurch, throwing the men flat on their faces in the slime, and then rose quickly to settle seemingly for good once more in the thick mud. As I pulled back the control column to prevent the aircraft from nosing over a violent gust threw the Gemini into the air. I found myself struggling to regain control without time even to glance at my friends clawing themselves out of the mire. Once airborne I prayed silently to myself, knowing what a prize boob I had made. But for the grace of God it could have been a very different ending.

Lympne was soon in sight and because of the strength of the wind I must have landed in about ten yards. I was thankful to reach the shelter of the high boundary trees to the south-east of the aerodrome.

Clearing customs and immigration in good time I took off cautiously and set course for a very rough ride to Marseille. Over France however the weather improved and following a relaxed overnight stop in Marseille I flew a faultless flight to Castel Benito in Libya. I found Castel Benito large, organised, efficient and under RAF control, so different from the prewar days of small landing strips along the coastline. When I asked for breakfast at midnight and a weather forecast extending as far as El Adem my demand engendered no surprise, only a request for me to attend the briefing. The young officer in the briefing room was not quite sure how to deal with me because as a civilian I did not require RAF flight plan approval. I put him at his ease by asking what he recommended, which was a mistake because he immediately advised against the direct route over so much water in a non-radio aircraft. I thanked him and said that this time I was using two engines where formerly I had only one.

Although the runways and perimeter tracks had coloured direction studs I switched on the landing light in the nose because there was still an enormous amount of impedimenta, collected no doubt from the surrounding battle area, placed uncomfortably close to the runway. I took off and, leaving the few lights of Tripoli behind me, climbed steadily on a direct course for El Adem, levelling out at 8,000 feet. The conditions were perfectly calm with the stars showing brilliantly against an almost black backcloth and I felt this was going to be a very easy and relaxed flight. I found that I could trim the Gemini so accurately on the elevator tabs that it would fly hour after hour at a constant height, plus or minus 20 feet, and that the compass needle could be kept spot-on track with occasional very slight pressure on the rudder. This left my hands free to study the maps with the aid of a flashlamp and to work out any navigational problems with my slide-rule.

I was fully absorbed in preparing my flight plan from Cairo onwards when my complacency was unexpectedly shattered. The smooth synchronised note of the engines changed and the aircraft suddenly yawed to port. This was a calamity I had not anticipated; it brought home to me very forcibly how over-confident and foolish one could get given the security of two engines as opposed to one. I did not yet know the Gemini sufficiently well to have confidence in its single-engine performance. Fortunately the aircraft was lightly loaded but nevertheless I was aware that it was impossible to maintain my present height.

Hundreds of miles out to sea in the black of night was not a comforting place to be with a failing engine. Moreover, in my mistaken confidence, I had omitted to put on board a life jacket or rubber dinghy for use in an occurrence such as this. I had nothing to keep me afloat and if the sea was really rough my chances of surviving until daylight to be picked up were

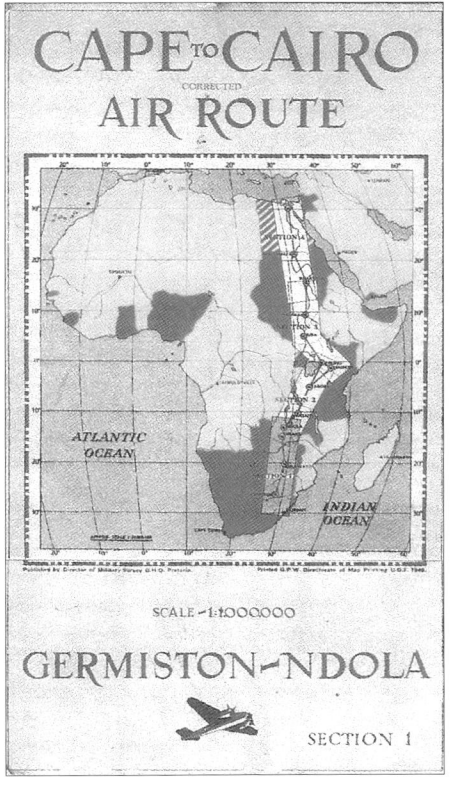

During his long-distance flights across Africa the author used maps to 1: 1,000,000 scale published by the Director of Military Survey, GHQ Pretoria in 1945. For flying between Cairo and Germiston separate maps divided the route into four stages. Illustrated here is the cover of the map for Stage One, from Germiston to Ndola.

This was the Miles Aerovan Mk 4 owned by D.B. Bruce. After Bruce's death the aircraft was sold and based in Beirut. On November 22, 1948 the Aerovan crashed at Rutbah Wells in Iraq and the wreck was taken to Baghdad.

*Aircraft designers Frederick George Miles (March 1903-August 1976)* **left***, and his brother George Herbert Miles (July 1911-September 1999),* **below***.* ***Right****, Miles test pilot Tommy Rose (January 1895-June 1968).*

*Miles M.65 Gemini 1A G-AISD was built at Woodley and received its Certificate of Airworthiness in April 1947. The author ferried this aircraft from Lympne to Germiston, Johannesburg in April 1947. Sold in Kenya as VP-KDH in June 1947, this Gemini spent many years flying in Belgium as OO-RLD, owned by Guy Valvekens. At the time of writing the aircraft was still airworthy. (Via Roger T. Jackson).*

slim. I had also been negligent in failing to bring water or emergency rations. Even assuming I struck the coastline, if the aircraft's performance was less than I hoped, there were hundreds of square miles of arid desert in between Arab settlements. Though I automatically checked the machine with rudder control following the loss of engine power, the port engine began surging badly and the luminous rev counter needle chased erratically around the indicator dial. On closing and opening the port throttle I found the engine would run only at maximum power. Although I did not have variable pitch propellers I thought I could keep the engine revolutions within safe limits if I reduced the power and speed by drawing back on the starboard engine. I needed all the power possible on the starboard engine to maintain height but care had to be taken to ensure it did not over-rev and perhaps fail. This was a sobering thought when the map indicated just how far out to sea and how far away from the local shipping lanes I was. Manipulating the throttles in the manner described worked well for a time, without undue discomfort other than a slight pressure required on the rudder controls. But then the smooth purr of the port engine once again reverted to a violent surging, so unpleasant that it was necessary to close it down completely. I was almost certain that the trouble was carburation but as the propeller now merely windmilled uselessly I pulled the Gemini up into a semi-stall, turned off the fuel to the port engine, flicked the switches off and brought the propeller to a stop.

Instinctively, with the first shock of the engine failure, I had already turned the machine south in an attempt to make for the North African shore. Calmer, and with a clearer mind, I checked my estimated position. I reckoned I was right in the centre of the Gulf of Sidra and that to carry on to Benghazi did not entail any more water crossing than a course to the south, or a return to Tripoli.

Although the Gemini was lightly loaded I could not maintain 8,000 feet in spite of the fact that I was now able to use full throttle on the starboard engine without over-revving. As the dim outline of the coast showed faintly below I was rather disturbed to find so few lights where I knew Benghazi to be. Moreover, I was unable to pick out the aerodrome. In the calm night air the Gemini was now purring happily on one engine and I was able to flatten out the prolonged glide in the descent. I now had the choice of either circling over Benghazi and losing precious height, in the hope that someone hearing my little engine would switch on the aerodrome lighting, or I could proceed on my direct course for El Adem. If I chose the latter, with the dawn light, I would be in a better position to deal with the situation, always assuming that I could remain airborne on one engine.

The black sky with fading stars now showed signs of a lighter blue on the eastern horizon. Soon narrow streaks of burning red gave warning of the birth of a new day. I could now see that what I had previously thought to be desert below was in fact stratus cloud. In places it was about 8/10ths but in large areas it completely obscured the ground. No doubt this was the reason why I had not been able to see Benghazi as clearly as I had expected.

I was now at 2,500 feet and with care the Gemini could be held above the level of the white carpet of cloud. With any attempt to gain altitude on one engine the aircraft immediately lost speed without any compensating benefit. I began to worry that I could be forced to land prematurely if the heat of the day became intense enough to impair the volumetric efficiency of the running engine. Thus, with the further loss of power, I would be compelled to increase the angle of attack, which in turn would induce so much drag that I would be forced to descend whatever lay beneath.

I was also unhappy about my navigation and dead reckoning and I thought wistfully about those pilots fortunate to have the luxury of a good radio. The variation in flying speed through the night brought about by the failure of the port engine was such that I could not rely upon an accurate judgement on which to work out the ground speed.

El Adem was small and almost indiscernible but a short distance away. Normally it would have been easy to lose height and then fly beneath the stratus that now obstructed any clear view of the desert ahead. In my present situation, though I knew the height of the top of the stratus I did not know how low it extended. If it formed part of the early morning fog, so prevalent in these conditions, if I so much as touched the cloud a crash-landing would be unavoidable. My best hope was to wait until I saw a clear patch so that the terrain could be studied more carefully in the hope that I had not overshot El Adem in the meantime.

My luck was in. After a very short spell the white carpet beneath ended momentarily and directly below was revealed the arid waste of the Libyan desert. As I peered intently to make out any cloud shadow that would give an indication of the height of the ground, I put the Gemini into a gentle right-hand turn. I was relieved to see almost stationary patchy dark shadows that were not fog but cloud breaking in the heat of the blazing sun. Moreover my spirits rose at once when ahead, in that vast expanse of flat desert, I saw some large buildings which could only be the RAF hangars at El Adem.

As I approached the aerodrome there was little or no activity, only a Dakota and an Avro York parked on the tarmac. The sun had by this time burnt up all the scudding cloud and I was conscious of the fact that I might soon be parked out in the blazing heat while I waited for someone to come out and diagnose the engine fault. With this in mind, and not relishing the prospect of a long walk from the perimeter of that sprawling aerodrome, I decided to risk the displeasure of the air traffic controller by putting the Gemini down as near to the apron and hangars as possible. With the confidence gained in the night, and help from what little height I had remaining, I put the Gemini into a steep turn to complete a full circuit, before lowering the undercarriage to touchdown to a standstill almost in line with the parked aircraft. I rested for a moment and thanked God for turning what could have been a painful and perhaps dramatic incident into what was now an enlivening experience.

The incident had an amusing side. As I opened the cockpit door I heard an RAF ground crew man shout to his mate: "Blimey, did you see that, 'Arry? What the hell does he want two engines for?"

Without any delay, and with the willing assistance from the RAF, we found the cause of the failure to be in the carburettor, a piece of cotton waste in the main jets, so large I marvelled how it had travelled so far without being trapped in the filter.

With the bit between my teeth I now wanted to get to Barbara and Alex as soon as I possibly could, so I set Wadi Halfa as my goal for the night. As I cleared Cairo the officials were friendly and courteous but so maddeningly slow it was two hours before I was able to set course over the long, green snake-like twisting River Nile.

As the huge ball of fire that was the sun sank slowly on the starboard wing, the sea of sand below changed to a fiery red before gradually turning to black. Prudence should have dictated making a landing in the fading light at Luxor, but I was now gaining such confidence with my little twin that I plotted a careful course for Wadi Halfa. Cool, calm and peaceful after the heat of the day, I sat back a little tired but relaxed. Ahead, the odd patch of reflected light indicated that another bend of the Nile was about to be crossed. As my ETA drew near I saw ahead the dull glow of Wadi Halfa. Heading the machine to the east of the town I switched on the landing light and pointed it at a small solitary line of lights that I correctly guessed was my destination, and in due course landed.

It had been my intention to proceed direct to Entebbe in the morning but, on landing at Khartoum, I was politely but firmly informed that I could not travel through the Sudan without radio, unless in convoy with another machine of similar performance. This would have been a frustrating and serious setback but fortunately I made contact with Capt. Kelly, an airline pilot who was flying on the route between Khartoum and Nairobi. He agreed to act as radio escort as far as Juba. It was all a little juvenile and quite futile, for after we had taken off before dawn the following day, neither of us saw the other until we met again in the Norfolk Hotel in Nairobi.

I had hoped to push on quickly south, but so much interest was shown in the Gemini that I was pressed to detour as far as Dar es Salaam in order to demonstrate it to the Director of Civil Aviation for Tanganyika, and also two directors of the firm Wigglesworth & Company, Messrs Adamson and Wallace.

Sweeping low over the Serengeti plains above the heads of herds of thundering wildebeest and zebra, avoiding the swirling dust devils and twisting between the tall sisal trees was a wonderful experience. The

Gemini was slow enough to permit me to safely observe wild life in a manner never before experienced. The small group awaiting me on the landing strip at Dar es Salaam was equally impressed with the Gemini and whilst they gave it full marks for safety, and were impressed with the single-engine performance, they were somewhat caustic about its wooden construction and the appetite of the ants!

In my anxiety to get an early start for Lusaka, which I hoped would be my final stop before reaching Johannesburg, I asked the young English officer in the wooden shed that served as a control tower and office if I might clear my paperwork that evening. He readily agreed, but when I told him I was going to fly direct to Lusaka he said that it was now impossible and that I must fly via Tabora. I protested that this would add at least another four hours to my flying time and I would be unable to complete the journey in a day.

In answer to this he said: "I have just received a new flight directive. The region between here and Lusaka is very mountainous, the country wild and inaccessible and we have no weather information for the route. I cannot stop you but I must report your departure to Tabora and Nairobi and I have no doubt that they will take further steps in the matter at a later date."

With this sobering admonishment in mind I sensed that the time was fast approaching when the freedom of the sky over Africa would succumb to the restricting control of bureaucracy, in promotion of safety and efficiency, that would mean the end of pilots like myself. I felt then that, if I had to go I would do so in the manner I always had. If and when the powers that be took away my licence, then at least in my own way I had enjoyed to the full the years of an era that I knew would never come our way again.

The next morning I took off alone and unaided. The hot sticky breeze from the sea gave promise of worse discomforts. As I climbed on to my direct course a bright glow towards Zanzibar told me that the sun was already on the move. It was not long before the clear blue sky filled up with huge towering cumulus clouds that darkened in precipitation further ahead and covered the mountain range that crossed my flight path. I had plenty of height to clear the highest peaks but nevertheless I coaxed another 2,000 feet from the Gemini before checking everything for the final time, bracing myself for the buffeting I felt sure was to come.

At first the unpleasant turbulence was more irritating and discomforting than I had experienced over the past few days. Then, with an abruptness that startled me, we struck a heavy and severe rainstorm in a crescendo of noise. This continued for a few minutes and then, as suddenly as it had begun, the staccato tattoo stopped and we passed from the black storm-cloud into a brilliant white mass. And so it continued; first a dark saturating downpour, followed by a violent buffeting in the thermals that the brighter cumulus seemed to produce.

After four hours, during a moment when I was wondering if I was still on course, the storm clouds divided below to reveal a mass of green water that could only be Lake Nyasa. Having just glimpsed the western shoreline of the lake I was able to work out precisely whether or not I had sufficient fuel to reach Lusaka. As near as I could tell the port engine was consuming 3.5 gallons per hour and the starboard 3.6. Providing that I ran out of the storm belt I should have enough fuel to reach my destination. I had barely completed all my calculations when breaks began to appear, and for the first time I could see a green blanket below, breaking up in parts, to reveal the familiar bush country away from the mountains.

I touched down at Lusaka in blazing sunshine after covering 966 statute miles in 8 hours and 20 minutes flying time. If the fuel gauges were accurate there was still sufficient fuel remaining for another hour's flying. I felt I had good reason to be satisfied with the little twin.

As expected, my landing at Johannesburg was a joyous occasion. Barbara and Alex were well and beaming with delight, as were the friends and visitors who greeted me on the arrival of an aircraft in which we had great expectations.

Later, when we had reached our home and were alone, Barbara confided: "Darling, I hate it here, when can we go home?" I began to tell her how I had found things in England. I also reminded her of the fact that I had agreed on a two-year contract when I joined the company. I concluded by saying: "It is a question of whether you want a dark cold winter or can stick a hot dry summer. I think if you had seen as much as I have seen in the past few weeks, you would prefer the hot dry summer for a while."

# Log of flight from Lympne to Germiston, April 4th–13th 1947 in Miles Gemini G-AISD

| Date | From | To | Time | | Remarks |
|------|------|-----|------|------|---------|
| April 4 | Lympne | Marseilles | 5 | 00 | |
| April 5 | Marseilles | Tunis | 3 | 40 | |
| " | Tunis | Castel Benito | 2 | 50 | |
| April 6 | Castel Benito | El Adem | 6 | 15 | Take off midnight |
| " | El Adem | Almaza | 3 | 46 | Landed at daybreak |
| " | Almaza | Wadi Halfa | 4 | 52 | |
| " | Wadi Halfa | Atbara | 2 | 58 | |
| April 7 | Atbara | Khartoum | 1 | 30 | |
| " | Khartoum | Juba | 6 | 20 | |
| April 9 | Juba | Entebbe | 3 | 12 | |
| " | Entebbe | Nairobi | 3 | 13 | |
| April 10 | Nairobi | Local flying | 1 | 30 | Demonstration |
| April 11 | Nairobi | Dar Es Salaam | 3 | 42 | |
| " | Dar Es Salaam | Local flying | 1 | 20 | Demonstration |
| April 12 | Dar Es Salaam | Lusaka | 8 | 20 | |
| April 13 | Lusaka | Bulawayo | 2 | 41 | |
| " | Bulawayo | Germiston | 4 | 00 | |
| | | **Total flying** | **65** | **09** | |

Two views showing the cockpit of the prototype Miles M.65 Gemini G-AGUS, complete with blind-flying panel. The Gemini's roomy cockpit was sound-proofed and well laid out with an excellent field of vision for the pilot and three passengers. On opposite sides of the pilot's seat can be seen the trim wheel and the hand-operated flap control. Production aircraft were fitted with retractable undercarriages. Both cabin doors could be jettisoned in the event of an emergency. (The Aeroplane photograph).

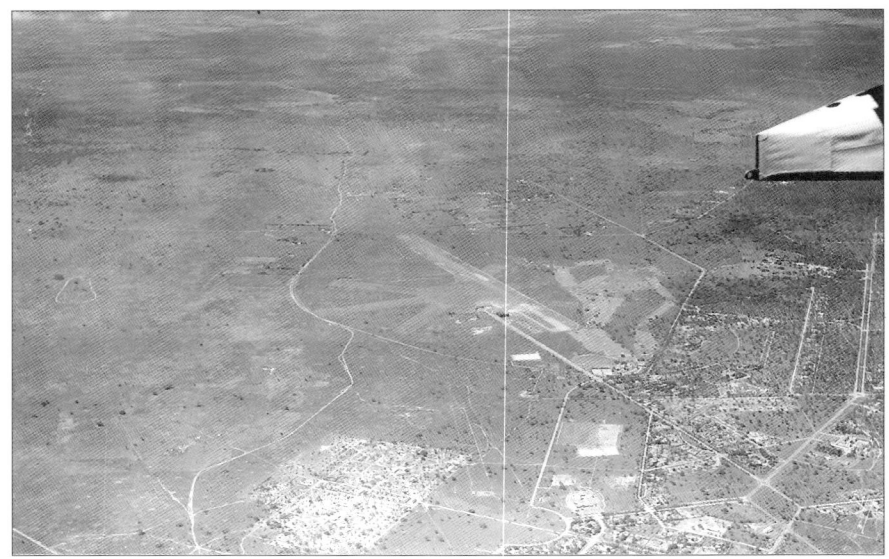

**Above**, *the airfield at Lusaka photographed from a Short Solent flying boat in May 1948.* (The Aeroplane photograph).

**Right,** *the author's son Alex waving at the camera at Luanda on July 3, 1947.* (Author).

**Below**, *Miles M.65 Gemini 1A ZS-BRV, in which the author made an extensive African sales tour during June and July 1947.* (via Roger T. Jackson).

**Above,** the author returns to Elizabethville in Gemini ZS-BRV after an engine failure necessitated a forced landing in wild country on the way to a Congo plantation near Bukama in June 1947. (Author).

**Below,** waiting to see the author off from Belvedere, Salisbury on June 28, 1947 are Mrs. Hensman and her two children. Holding her hand is the author's son Alex. A BOAC Avro York can be seen being refuelled in the background. (Author).

*This photograph shows the author in the right-hand seat of Gemini ZS-BRV warming up the engines just prior to leaving Elizabethville on July 1, 1947. (Author).*

*Watched by the locals Barbara and son Alex shelter from the scorching sun whilst they open the picnic basket beneath the port wing of the Miles Gemini ZS-BRV at Vila Luso in July 1947. (Author).*

# CHAPTER 8

# A FATE WORSE THAN DEATH

Notwithstanding the fact that our disenchantment with Johannesburg had now become total and irreversible, I should be a hypocrite if I did not acknowledge that there were times when I was totally captivated by what this wonderful land had to offer. Such occasions included motoring with Barbara and Alex along smooth wide roads in the glistening luxurious comfort of the new Packard. The sheer beauty of those magnificent long broad avenues, cloaked in the delicate mauve veil of the jacaranda trees against a sky so blue, seemed unreal. The enormous bustling shops displayed an astonishing and fantastic variety of tempting products unheard of and as yet unseen in postwar Europe. Even Barbara had to admit that we could be far worse off at home, and of course Alex revelled in it all.

Most of our friends in South Africa allowed their children to be fed, clothed and literally brought up by their nannies. Even when on holiday they would leave them to the care of trusted and well-trained staff. We had never done this and Alex went with us wherever possible with the result that a very close, frank and honest trust developed between the three of us. I am not certain that this may have been overdone so early in his life. Often, when in conversation with Barbara, I was unaware of Alex's presence, particularly in the car when he would stand behind us, his arms resting on the back of my seat, taking in every word that was said. One day we were driving in the relaxed atmosphere of the city when a car cut in front of us in a dangerous manner. Before I could say anything a small calm voice from the back exclaimed: "Dozy bastards haven't got a clue, have they, Dad?" Barbara and I sat in silence with tears of laughter.

Some of the happiest and often hilarious times were spent at weekends with the Albus and their young, boisterous but endearing children on the Pienards River farm some miles north of Pretoria. Here Major Sholto Douglas sometimes joined us and time was spent riding and shooting, or just lazing round the improvised pool. The riding was not always a soft hacking trot. The Albu's eldest child, Georgina, was old enough and sufficiently well-schooled to handle a spirited mount, so that we often tore over the sun-baked ground, twisting left and right as the tracks wound through the tall bush. If a low-hanging branch brushed you off you were expected to catch your mount and vault on again at the gallop.

Best of all I liked the warm nights, when we would drive the big estate car and go off shooting hares. These were not hares as I knew them but larger members of the rodent family. They bred rapidly and were looked upon as a pest. With their strong and rather ugly hindquarters they could leap across the ground rapidly rather in the manner of a kangaroo. When,

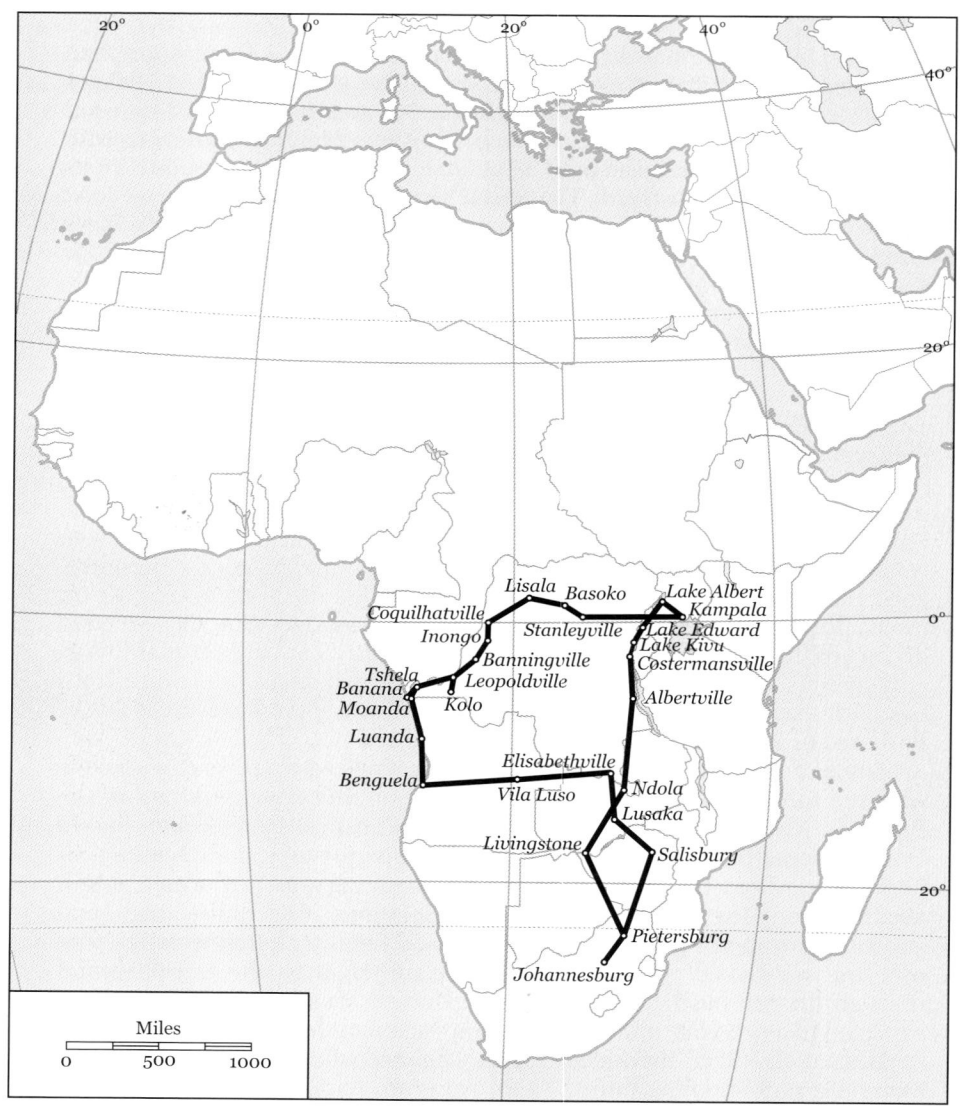

The route of the author's sales tour,
flown in Miles Gemini ZS-BRV from Johannesburg in June–July 1947.

with a broad grin, Sir George gave me a 12-bore gun and invited me to sit on the polished wing of the car, I had some idea of what I might expect. With this in mind I wrapped one leg around a headlamp and wedged my other foot into the front bumper bar. As we dodged frantically around over the rough ground I could hear those enjoying the comparative comfort of their cars shouting words of encouragement as I hung on like a bucking bronco. This was an exciting sport, blazing away with snap shots as spring hares darted in and out of the headlight beams, the tussocks of grass or maize stacks throwing moving shadows which did nothing to aid the man with the gun.

Our new Gemini attracted a great deal of interest. It basically fulfilled the requirement of a safe, cheap and reliable light aircraft and could fly long distances over forbidding territory, although it had obvious shortcomings, which I did not advertise. Nevertheless, as I now knew from personal experience, the little twin instilled great confidence in a pilot crossing jungle and desert, of which Africa had more than its fair share. The Belgian Congo seemed to present an ideal sales opportunity for the promising machine and it was proposed that I would make the first big tour with the particular objective of surveying a new delivery route from the UK via Entebbe, Stanleyville and Leopoldville. I planned my sales tour carefully but after our last experience I did not like the idea of leaving Barbara and Alex behind, despite the fact that both Ian Hay and George Albu would have been pleased for them to join their families during my absence. Alex was eager to come with me and Barbara considered that it *might* be a good idea. After giving the matter careful consideration I realised that taking a small family across the worst flying country in the world would be the best possible way of demonstrating confidence in the Gemini.

We left Germiston on June 27th 1947, but got off to a bad start. My chief mechanic had been keen to fit the Gemini with radio but in doing so had run into a number of snags. As my flying schedule was planned to within minutes I was compelled to tell him to take out the radio to allow me to proceed on my way. After a flight of five hours we arrived in Salisbury tired, disgruntled and late. All those who had planned to meet us at the aerodrome had long gone home fed up with waiting. Just as we were unloading though, our friends Mr and Mrs Hensman dropped in.

On arriving at the aerodrome the next morning I found the Gemini the object of great interest, surrounded by a number of keen, shrewd and intelligent aviators, who had news of my visit. After demonstrating the machine to a number of likely customers I took the Director of Civil Aviation, Maurice Barber, for a short flight before returning to Barbara and Alex, who were waiting impatiently on the tarmac to proceed on our way to Lusaka.

To me, Northern and Southern Rhodesia were the most wonderful countries in the world from a flying point of view. The weather for the most part is superb, with fantastic visibility. Though the vast bush lands extended for thousands of miles, the onset of boredom could be quickly dispelled by periods of very low flying, picking out the wide variety of wildlife as yet undisturbed by the encroachment of man. In all the years that I travelled this endearing land I cannot recall anything less than a warm welcome at every aerodrome or strip that I visited.

The Director of Civil Aviation, Muspratt Williams, and his charming wife greeted us at Lusaka. They drove us to their attractive residence, not far from the airfield, and in no time it was almost as though we had been one large happy family.

Belgium had always adopted a responsible attitude in its outlook concerning flying in the Congo, no doubt brought about by common sense. Because of the vast distances and inaccessible terrain the country's vast natural wealth was as yet untapped, thus precluding any development other than that which could be reached by aircraft. The work and progress with numerous well-kept airstrips in what otherwise would have been inaccessible terrain did the Belgians great credit even if, at that stage, the whole was economically not viable. Only those who have experienced the terrors of flying over endless steaming jungle and the sudden unpredictable storms can appreciate what it means to find a haven of safety within striking distance when all had seemed lost.

Elisabethville was no *dorp* in the Bundu and was blessed with a fine airport, good roads and a gracious way of living. We stayed in a modern comfortable hotel and from here I made my first sale of the tour, though really the Gemini sold itself. Mr Camelbec was a pleasant and humorous planter; he had insisted that I fly him over his cotton, palm and cattle plantations, which suited me very well as Alex had a slight temperature, and Barbara said she would take the opportunity to have a rest and catch up on some of her chores.

While Camelbec was flying the Gemini and describing how he had nearly been killed flying his de Havilland Puss Moth, the Gemini's port engine suddenly misfired badly and stopped. After turning off the port petrol tank and stopping the propeller from windmilling, I asked Camelbec which was the best forced-landing strip to make for, bearing in mind that we should need to carry out repairs before taking off again. He indicated with a pencil a point on the map, and I altered course without delay, very much aware that both the Gemini and I were on trial. When we arrived overhead the landing strip it appeared to be covered in long grass. I knew that once I was committed for a touchdown I would not be able to change my mind. Whilst we were floating along quite smoothly in level flight there was no way I was going to be able to climb out of the strip and over the surrounding tall trees on one engine. Peering down intently I made two low circuits. When Camelbec assured me it was all right I closed the starboard throttle and we touched down, the coarse grass turning out to be considerably smoother than it looked.

There was no ground engineer or mechanic available on the strip, only curious natives and a weather-beaten Belgian seated on an ancient tractor. I examined the Gemini's port engine carefully and soon found the cause of the trouble. My own mechanic, when attempting to screen the distributors for the radio installation, had cracked one of them, causing an electrical short.

Fortunately the man on the tractor produced a small drill from his crude toolkit and I was able to make a temporary repair. Once in the air again we continued on our way to Camelbec's place at Kasambo. There I was able to take a keen interest in all the various products grown and produced by the Camelbec organisation. Camelbec was in high spirits and on our return to Elisabethville was full of praise for the Gemini and looking forward to taking delivery.

With Alex now fit we planned an early start for our long flight to the West Coast the following day, July 2nd. After setting off, the flight was uneventful but proved to be tedious at such a low cruising speed. Our midway stop at Vila Luso was blisteringly hot with no shelter, so that Barbara and Alex crouched under the Gemini's wings for what little protection they could find. Meanwhile I hurried the refuelling along, perspiring uncomfortably under my pith helmet. Both engines started at the press of the button but then, on take-off, both faded and stopped completely. With the excessive heat I guessed the trouble must be a vapour lock and it was more than half an hour before I could clear the stoppage, during which time we slowly roasted. Off again we seemed to have been in the air for days rather than hours, so that the first glimpse of a faint coastline was more than welcome to us. The sun, a burning ball of fire, was sinking slowly to cast a dull glow over the calm Atlantic waters.

We circled over the small town of Benguela and, after touching down on the tiny level sand strip, we climbed somewhat dishevelled from our cramped little cockpit. As we did so we were astonished to be met by a welcoming committee of dozens of laughing, boisterous but well-behaved families with their children. It must have been a rare event for a visiting aircraft to land at such a remote spot, because the reception we received was so warm and spontaneous as to be embarrassing. Many British recall that the Portuguese are our oldest allies, but nearly always in a ribald manner. For my part I shall ever be indebted to them, for it was these kind people who kept the fires alight so that I was able to find Mossamedes in fog and darkness when I thought I was lost during the Cape record flight in February 1939.

As we took our luggage from the aircraft these people, of all ages, flooded round us. Streams more poured onto the open airstrip, ranging from pale Europeans to the blackest Negro; I guessed the whole town had come out to meet us. As the bags were taken from our hands it became a little overwhelming. We were shepherded over the sandy ground to our hotel, a short distance from where the Gemini was left overnight. We approached the hotel over a large track of dry dusty fine sand. The sand had blown up into small heaps and filtered on to the slatted wooden stoop that formed the front of the building. We were given the best suite available on the ground floor, though for a hotel that was little more than a shed with a rusty tin roof this may sound rather grand. We were very tired and, after a simple shower in what can only be described as primitive conditions, we settled for a plain meal, and after putting Alex to bed Barbara and I started to undress. Suddenly Barbara put on her robe and pointed to the open window, to where a row of faces had appeared. Yet more faces emerged and we were offered baskets of fruit, bowls of shrimps and prawns together with other strange-looking sea delicacies that these kind uninhibited people had caught and cooked especially for us. In order not to give any offence we ate as much as we could and then indicated that we were very tired and wanted to go to sleep. Not a bit of it! Finding us friendly the Portuguese rushed off to find other members of their families, and in no time at all we must have had half the town squatting outside our window all anxious to talk, though none of us could understand a thing that was said. By this time we were nearly dropping, but there was no denying these friendly and charming people. In the end Barbara and I got into bed to a chorus of chatter coming through the open window. The more daring were now attempting snatches of broken English or French. Eventually I fell asleep, a sea of faces grinning at me from the window, aware that Barbara had already dropped off.

In the morning our new-found friends returned in smaller numbers to watch our departure. I drove with our main hosts in a battered car to demonstrate the Gemini while Barbara and Alex trooped off with many willing followers to bathe in the sea and from the beautiful beach watch the local fishermen at work.

Again, I did not have to try and sell the Gemini; the enthusiastic little flying club bought it even before I flew it for them. The only problem was that they did not have any money. Such was their excitement and enthusiasm for the tiny twin that mere lack of funds was not going to be allowed to stand in their way. It was amusing to watch them as they fell into small groups, each hatching out some grandiose scheme to raise the necessary funds. I listened to their bright ideas and took down the specifications they required for their machine, but soon realised with some sadness that these pipe dreams would never materialise.

With some difficulty and with great regret we left these people the next day. They genuinely did not want us to leave and as we circled low over the smiling faces and waving hats it was to realise how simple and content life can be away from the stress, complexities and falseness that modern civilisation can bring.

During the flight northwards, following the coast beyond Luanda, I taught Alex, after some practice, to take the controls and hold the Gemini in level flight and gently turn with the curves of the surf beaten-beach below.

Our old friend Albert Fischer was waiting to greet us at his small well-kept airstrip at Moanda as we dived low from the mighty mouth of the dirty, stinking Congo. In addition to his holiday home built on this attractive cliff overlooking both the Atlantic and the Congo, Fischer had also built several appealing bungalows that were available for his guests. I suspected that he loved this place more than he was prepared to admit.

Meals at the Fischers were always an event and, as Barbara said, unbelievable in darkest Africa. As far as I could tell we were the only Europeans for miles. The domestic staff were all black and went about their work quite unobtrusively. They did not wear smart uniforms as in some of the more sophisticated homes in the Transvaal, but were quiet and efficient at their jobs and the quality of the food they prepared was beyond reproach. A typical meal would start with half a grapefruit, at least six inches across and so sweet that no sugar was required, with a flavour never experienced in England. This would be followed by a course of fish from the Atlantic or freshwater fish from the river, served with a chilled Hock or Moselle. Next could be a juicy thick steak from a Hereford or Aberdeen Angus, served with claret or a burgundy. Always there was a variety of desserts and I think the fresh strawberries were first choice. Cheese was served with biscuits but I liked best the fresh oven-baked bread, crisp golden on the outside and pure white as it was cut open. Old brandy or port with delicious coffee usually rounded off a remarkable evening, all within the sound of animals seeking their own meals in the untamed jungle.

With the drastic shortages in the early postwar Europe I was puzzled as to how Fischer managed to obtain wine of such excellent quality. He told me that he made large shipments of timber and other commodities from Matadi to the Americans, and that part of his agreement, made during the war, was that he could ask for almost anything. At times he made this request literally and if there was any undue delay, say for a refrigerator, car or food, he would merely delay shipment of American consignments until such time as his requirements had been fulfilled.

My next appointment was to have been with Baron de Rosee at his plantation at Tshela some distance in the jungle to the east. As the landing strip was so narrow and the trees tall and dense, it could easily be missed, so Fischer offered to show me the way. We left Barbara to rest and enjoy the sea on the small shore that nestled below the shallow beach.

We flew low over unbroken impenetrable foliage so dense that, peer as I might, it was difficult to see any sign of life below. Occasionally a few brightly-coloured birds would dart for better cover and at times I thought I saw apes or monkeys. Although we referred to 'darkest Africa,' there was nothing to associate this with the luxurious residence of the de Rosees. The landing strip was small and well-kept and adequate for light aircraft, and the house was solidly and beautifully constructed out of some of the country's finest timber. As we stepped from the aircraft a smart uniformed native conducted us up the wide wooden steps to the main reception room, which was elevated to give a pleasant view of the airstrip and part of the jungle.

Fischer, who knew the de Rosees well, introduced me to the Baroness, a very well dressed lady who had quietly entered the room as we walked in. She apologised for the absence of her husband, explaining that he was overdue returning from Leopoldville with some important government officials. Drinks were served and we sat down in a very comfortable open study adjoining the sitting room. From where I sat I could see a table laid as if for a banquet, with white wine already chilled in silver ice buckets and red wine being decanted by native staff. I quickly drank my grapefruit juice, realising that our presence was embarrassing the Baroness, who continually glanced out of the window as if expecting to see her husband's car coming up the drive. I thanked her and said to Fischer that we must return as I had promised Barbara that we would not be late. Out of politeness the Baroness asked us to have another drink, but instead of refusing and taking our leave Fischer, who was enjoying the situation, gave me a sly wink and settled further into his chair to enjoy another whisky. The Baroness then passed me a beautiful gold inlaid guest book and asked me if I would sign it before leaving. As I thumbed through the pages I saw that the entry on the first page was: 'Albert, King of the Belgians, January 5th 1912.' I politely handed back the book and said to Fischer very pointedly that we must take our leave.

Bowing to the Baroness he replied: "There's no hurry, I always enjoy the charming company at Tshela; we'll have another drink and then get on our way." By the time we had finished our third drink it was getting late and Fischer, with a twinkle in his eye, said: "I think your guests must have broken down and will probably not arrive until tomorrow. It's a pity that such a lovely lunch should be wasted."

The poor Baroness hesitated and then replied: "I suppose you are right, we may as well eat it, it is bound to be ruined anyway." To my acute embarrassment Fischer took her at her word and without hesitation got up and walked with her into the dining room, where discreet and very competent native staff were awaiting expectantly. I felt very sorry for the Baroness for the dilemma in which she now found herself. Though the atmosphere as the meal commenced was cool, polite and a little frigid, Fischer was enjoying every moment of the situation. However, the quality of the food and wine soon relaxed us all and in no time our charming hostess had forgotten the irritations of the morning and was asking me about Barbara, Guy de Chateaubrun and his connections with the Belgian Royal Family.

She was about to tell me an amusing story of their early life in the Congo when the sound of a car horn caused her to give a startled gasp and she almost leapt out of her chair. The noise of a powerful car engine being revved at high speed heralded the arrival of her husband and three guests, who bustled into the room full of apologies, explaining how a large tree had fallen across the narrow road and that it had taken time to find sufficient manpower to remove it. As the group turned expectantly towards the dining table, now not quite so trim and immaculate, the Baroness looked on speechless. Not so Fischer – he thought it was all a huge joke and said as much to de Rosee and his companions. He was still laughing as we climbed out of the Gemini at Moanda, where Barbara and Alex were waiting impatiently for us to arrive.

We spent several days on the mouth of the Congo and Albert Fischer saw to it that we were never bored. I also made many trips into Leopoldville and the interior to my old friend van Lancker at Kolo. Finally, in order to make amends for our previous behaviour, I paid another visit to the de Rosees, taking Barbara and Alex with me. I was surprised when both the Baron and his wife burst out laughing on recalling the previous incident, regarding it as a marvellous story and having received much amusement in telling it to their friends.

On July 9th 1947 we started on our way to Entebbe, via Stanleyville and the rainy forest. Knowing that this could be the most dangerous flying sector in Africa I made my flight plan with care, using a track that would keep me in comfortable reach of emergency landing strips wherever possible. The first leg to Banningville was for the most part flown over broken country with the occasional village, and the journey was uneventful and easy. From Banningville to Inongo the terrain began to change and we soon began to encounter vast areas of impenetrable jungle. Through the dank undergrowth we caught the occasional reflection of the overhead sun on a flooded clearing.

On arriving at Coquilhatville we were somewhat startled to find great activity, with troops and aircraft rapidly dispersing around the airfield. As field guns and ammunition tenders were moved into prepared positions I thought for a moment that a crisis had broken out and that an attack was imminent. As I taxied to a standstill our fears were soon allayed. We were met by a highly-polished camouflaged Jeep, its metalwork glistening in the sun, driven by an upright driver whose appearance approximated polished ebony.

From the Jeep stepped an immaculate Belgian army officer, resplendent in gold braid, snow-white uniform and helmet. After asking who we were and the purpose of our visit, he apologised and asked if we would mind waiting with our aircraft at the end of the airfield until the Prince Regent, who was making an inspection of military forces in the Congo, had landed. As we saw the approaching Douglas Dakota glinting in the sun frenzied activity broke out all over the airfield. Officers shouted commands to the various forces to take up their ceremonial positions. My only regret was that I did not have a ciné-camera with colour film with which to record the brilliance of the scene that began to unfold. The Regent and the Royal Party stepped down the sparkling aluminium aircraft stairs, their white and gold uniforms contrasting with the red fez-type hats and khaki uniforms of the jet-black troops that had formed the guard of honour. There followed a long walk to inspect the shining field guns drawn up parallel to the gravel runway. White flags waved in the hot gentle breeze, a black band struck up and the whole airfield came to life as the parade moved at a spanking pace past the Prince Regent to a never-to-be-forgotten tune of the First World War. Although we did not know it at the time, this was probably the last time that a member of the Belgian Royal Family would make an inspection of military forces in such a remote part of the Congo.

While this most interesting interruption to our activities was going on I had taken the opportunity to study carefully the map for the next leg of our flight, to Stanleyville. It would have been easy for me to fly in a direct line from Coquilhatville, but we were now entering country that had fewer emergency landing strips and where a safe landing outside a recognised airfield would have been impossible. Prudence demanded that I fly a longer route via Lisala and Basoko, even though the visibility and flying conditions were perfect.

We landed at Stanleyville in time to explore this most fascinating of towns in the Congo. Later in life, when Barbara and I reflected on our experiences in Africa, there was little doubt in our minds that Stanleyville portrayed Africa as it had been for thousands of years. Even the traumatic impact of commercial exploitation and white supremacy appeared to have had made little impact. As we walked along the well-worn banks of the enormous mass of water that was the Congo, with the sun sinking out of sight and the heat haze rising from the steaming jungle, this impression only deepened. With Alex between us we stood entranced as we watched some long shallow canoes row past. We continued watching until we could no longer see the flashing oars, but only hear the soft harmonious chants as the Negroes forced their unstable craft through those deep and often turbulent currents that ultimately led to the Atlantic. We might have been in another world.

The night was now dark and mist and haze dimmed any light from the stars, yet the trees, bushes and the grass all around appeared to be glowing in an unbelievable manner. It was like a picture taken from fairyland and then as Alex shouted with delight the glow went out and left dark Cimmerian patches, so that the trees and bushes now blended into the night. We kept quiet for a while and the magical glow returned as myriad glow-worms cautiously exposed their tiny phosphorescent lamps once more. We walked along the riverbank in silence holding hands. Mingled with the chanting of the native paddlers was the incessant background

The author turns over the starboard propeller of Miles Gemini ZS-BRV prior to a flight from the Fischer's strip at Moanda in July 1947 – son Alex can be seen in the cockpit. Albert Fischer's Miles Messenger OO-CCM can be seen in the background. (Author).

The Henshaw family with Albert Fischer in front of Gemini ZS-BRV during a stay at the Fischer's summer residence at Moanda, on the mouth of the Congo, in July 1947. (Author).

**Above,** *Prince Regent Charles of Belgium boards his Dakota at Coquilhatville to continue his tour of the Belgian Congo - July 10, 1947. (Author).*

**Right,** *the author chats to the Belgian Prince Regent's assistant at Coquilhatville whilst waiting for the Prince to board the Dakota seen in the background - July 10, 1947.* (Author).

**Below,** *the scene at Stanleyville on July 11, 1947. As the refuelling bowser is pushed away the Henshaws start loading their luggage into the nose of Gemini ZS-BRV. In the background can be seen a Sabena DC-4. (Author).*

noise of crickets, interspersed with harsher squeals and screams from the jungle. Then, at odd times, there was a surge and splash of water close by as a disturbed crocodile slid deep into the dark depths at the foot of the bank on which we walked. To the swishswish of the paddles and the deep chant of the natives we strolled back to our simple quarters and prepared ourselves for the flight to Entebbe the next day.

At that time the route over the rainy forest, for obvious reasons, was little used. In fact I had never come across anyone who had flown over it. I had however known several people who had travelled or lived near the region and I was well prepared to treat every aspect of the flight with caution and respect. I had assured Barbara that I would not leave Stanleyville unless the weather forecast for the entire route was reassuring. I soon discovered that obtaining a weather report due east was impossible, and for once I found the few Belgian officials disinterested and unhelpful. The weather however was lovely and having had days of perfect flying conditions in the Congo we decided to leave as soon as I had refuelled and carefully checked the aircraft.

With Alex settled happily with his toys in the back of the Gemini we took off for Entebbe on July 11th. I was not going to take any chances and I put the machine into a long steady climb to 10,000 ft. After carefully checking the compass we all settled down for a long flight in perfect conditions. There was nothing to watch but the vast sea of green jungle that stretched in all directions as far as the eye could see. Barbara and I relaxed, as Alex became absorbed with a jigsaw puzzle.

We had flown for about two and a half hours in perfect calm when we struck one or two sharp bumps and I told Barbara to make sure that Alex's seat-straps were tight. The weather was still very good but the earlier gin-clear skies had now started to cloud over in patches. I noticed that some heavier black weather cloud had formed both behind as well as in front of us. During all this time we had not once seen a clearing, a native village or even a track. There was only the monotonous carpet of dark green jungle, devoid even of the mighty Congo that would at least have given a reassuring approximation to our position on the map.

In planning the flight I had calculated to intercept at Irumu the one and only track running from Stanleyville to Entebbe. Though this was a little north of our track it kept us safely west of the impassable Rwanda mountain range. A slight change of course at this point should lead us easily to our destination, via the southern tip of Lake Albert. When this track failed to show up at the dead reckoning time I reasoned that it was lost in the dense jungle below, in which case we would be unable to pick it out. By this time the cloud was forcing me to lose height and I was getting anxious for any fix that would confirm our exact position. Barbara and I studied the map carefully and then peered below. Suddenly, at the same instant, we spotted two large rivers twisting like black snakes and then blending together to form what I thought was a distinct junction. This was a perfect point on which to determine our true position. But it proved to be more difficult than I had expected; my estimated calculations in no way fitted into the fix on the map. What was even more disturbing was that a river junction exactly the shape and size of the one we could see below could be seen clearly on the map, only it showed us to be a hundred miles off course. I checked and cross-checked my original calculations and finally examined the compass and looked for anything we might inadvertently have placed near the instrument.

There was nothing and in the end I said to Barbara: "It's no use, I've checked everything. Either this map is inaccurate or we are way off course; God only knows where we shall finish up." I decided to remain firm on the original compass course whilst I mulled over the possibilities. I wondered if the compass had been disturbed in any way. My last check on the flight from Basoko to Stanleyville had indicated that the maps and compass were accurate. By the time I had considered the various possibilities point by point, including whether to turn back on a direct reciprocal course, the weather had taken a dramatic turn for the worse. The sun had completely disappeared and ahead I could see heavy rain. I half-turned the Gemini with the intention of returning, only to see that heavy black storms had developed behind us. Having passed the halfway stage I decided without hesitation that it was better to continue on course. I was very worried that after three hours in the air the only map check I had been able to make had put us so far off course. The more I thought about it the more I thought the maps were wrong. The only other explanation was that by sheer coincidence we had happened to pick out two rivers that matched those we should have been over but could not see because of the dense undergrowth.

The uncertainty was so unsettling I finally asked Barbara to pass me the world atlas I invariably carried on long trips. Though less detailed it showed more of Africa than the strip map I was using. The atlas showed very clearly the high Ruwenzori Range, better known to novelists as the Mountains of the Moon. This was to the south of our track, whereas the fix we thought we had found was well to the north and would have placed us in a wild region without habitation or a landing ground and no obvious means of knowing our whereabouts until too late.

Turning to Barbara I said: "I am not at all happy; I don't think I dare turn back and I am not sure where we are, but I am going to ignore the fix we saw and work out another dead-reckoning position. In order to confirm it I'll work out another course that, if I am right, will put us near this range of mountains. We'll know when we reach them because they'll be too high to cross."

By this time the rain had become torrential. Lightning was ripping the dark clouds with blue and yellow gashes and from time to time we would see a plume of steam and smoke below where it had struck the ground.

Each flash was followed almost immediately by a vibrating roll of thunder that could be heard above the noise of the engines, and the constant drumming as the deluge outside cascaded down upon us. Alex was chattering away in the back as the little Gemini bucked in the sky. First his topee was flung from his head and then he excitedly tried to catch his toys as they were continually thrown from the seat and the cockpit floor. With each violent surge the toys leapt up in front of his face and he made giggling attempts to catch them before they fell back to the floor. I whispered to Barbara to make sure his seat harness was tight. When I asked him if he was alright he replied: "Yes, Daddy, I'm fine but these naughty toys will not stay still."

Barbara looked me in the eye and without a word she knew I was becoming desperately worried. While concentrating on the controls I had not spoken to her but she had seen me increase the power several times so that I now had both engines at full throttle. In the tropical deluge my main concern had been the possibility of the wooden propellers disintegrating. So far they seemed to be standing up to the demands very well, but now a more sinister aspect of the flight had become apparent. I had held my altitude for as long as the storm clouds would allow but, as the conditions worsened, I had been forced to lose height. I was now flying a few feet above the solid mass of tree-tops at full throttle, looking and praying for a track or village to show up. As if it was not bad enough flying hour after hour seeing nothing but dense jungle, the torrential rain slowly but surely intensified. I became aware that the longitudinal trim of the machine was gradually altering and that I needed more power to maintain the same height. This lasted for what seemed hours and I sweated out the agonising realisation in silence.

Barbara and I always had telepathic perception and I knew that she would sense what I was suffering. To ease my distress she put her hand on my shoulder and then turned to Alex as she did so. Alex had stopped playing with his toys and although not upset by the constant buffeting he nevertheless sensed that something was wrong. He remained very quiet and as still as the never-ending bucking would allow. I prayed earnestly and desperately, hoping to spot in the unbroken jungle below a track of any sort, or a village where I could crash-land before it was too late.

Although flying full throttle on both engines I was horrified to realise that we were slowly but surely losing altitude. It would now be only a matter of time before I would be forced on to the tops of the trees in a stalled crash landing. As far as the flying was concerned there was no decision to make, that was a forgone conclusion that was now out of my hands. My agony of mind was rested with a plan of action when the final act took place. I sweated and prayed to myself, knowing in my heart that I must face the fact that there was little time left. I must not show my fear and distress to Alex. Barbara knew what I was going through and I knew she was waiting for me to put it into words.

I told her: "I'm afraid we are losing out on this, I don't know how we shall finish up when we hit the trees. If I am alright you can leave it to me but if not, the gun is in my right side pocket." She leaned over and kissed me and said: "It may not be that bad, we can probably make it to a village or something and if we survive the impact someone will find us if we hang on long enough."

I replied: "It's no good kidding ourselves, if we get away with the landing the only thing that will find us will be the ants; don't let Alex suffer." She turned to Alex, now very quiet and aware that something terrible was happening, and put her arms around him. A feeling of remorse welled up inside me, I felt I would choke. I now realised that I never should have brought my wife on such a flight. Though I had taken every precaution I had fallen into the trap like some novice pilot.

I did not have excessive loading on the elevators, but the serious decrease in speed had put the little machine in such a steep climbing attitude that the angle of attack of the wings induced such excessive drag that we were not climbing at all. I had to lose height in order to maintain flying speed. The situation was exacerbated by the fact that the air was like a blast from a furnace and impaired the volumetric efficiency of the engines. Also, had I been flying at sea-level, I would have had some increase in power output. But here, although we were almost touching the treetops, the altimeter was reading nearly 4,000 ft above sea level.

In the relentless downpour we both strained our eyes trying to pick out even the slightest break or clearing in the sea of green below. The perspiration poured from my face and neck in a dirty stream onto my badly-soiled bush shirt. I was suffering in silence the agony of the damned amidst a cacophony of noise. Although the force and weight of water striking the Gemini sounded like a thousand kettledrums playing in a small room, it had gone on for so long neither Barbara or I were aware of it. Because the Gemini's large windscreen had been obscure since the storms began we had been using the small sliding side windows, ignoring the water that cascaded with the slipstream into our faces. But now we were not only flying at full throttle, the aircraft was now reaching its critical angle of attack. The situation was not helped by the fact that, although both throttles were opened wide, the revolutions had dropped because the fixed-pitch propellers had also slowed up with our gradual decrease in flying speed.

Disaster could now be only a matter of minutes away. Waves of panic swept over me and only the physical demands to prevent the Gemini from flicking into a final stall kept my mind sufficiently concentrated on the job in hand. Had the turbulence continued with the onset of the storms I would certainly have lost control much earlier. The irony now was that, although the air had become comparatively calm, our fate was to be the same.

Barbara gently rested her head on my shoulder and I think we must have silently prayed together. Never taking my eyes away from the small window on my left, I began to judge where the end would come. At that moment I was aware of a dark outline of grey cloud amidst the continuous deluge ahead. It was barely distinguishable from the gloom around us and, believing that I was only kidding myself, I said nothing about it to Barbara. Suddenly she gripped my arm and pointed slightly ahead to the right and looked at me questioningly. Hanging on desperately, with every nerve in my body tensed with fear and concentration, I realised that what we saw was not an illusion. At that moment I realised that the Gemini had flattened out very slightly and that, almost imperceptibly, the needle of the airspeed indicator had crept up on the dial. Bolstered by a renewed hope we both peered eagerly through the open windows and saw a softer streak of light some distance ahead that appeared to be a definite horizon, the first we had seen for hours. I tried to moisten my dry mouth and lips. Despite constant perspiring they felt like parchment; my tongue felt as though it did not belong to me.

Slowly the rain began to abate and holding Alex's hands Barbara and I mouthed a silent prayer. At that moment we both saw below a narrow parting in the otherwise unmarked jungle, and then a long straight narrow track which showed signs of use by vehicles. My immediate reaction was to land there and then and damn the consequences, but as I carefully circled I was sure that, though I might land without causing too much damage, I would never be able to fly the machine out again. There was no sign of life but I decided to keep the track in view. We followed it without difficulty until it suddenly disappeared into the tall trees and became lost in the dense undergrowth.

After our agonising ordeal I was not sure now what to do. Although the rain had stopped the weather was still far from good. I fervently hoped that the track we had just seen was the one and only route into Entebbe. I had not struck the Ruwenzori Range as planned but then our speed had been so slow that my original calculations would be all awry. I decided to stick to my course until we reached those high mountains; even though they would surely bar our way they would at least confirm our position on the map. We were more than thankful that not only were we back to normal cruising speed with a little height in hand, but at that moment we could see the clouds were brightening and taking on definite shapes. In some places the sun even appeared to be breaking through.

I was watching these lighter patches on the horizon when my spirits suddenly sank. Ahead I saw a darker mass that gave portent of another violent storm. Somehow it looked different as the partially broken cloud swirled around. Then, suddenly, the sun broke through with a penetrating beam and there, silhouetted sharply against a background of deep blue sky, stood the very mountain range that I had noted in the atlas some hours earlier. My hunch had been proved. The awesome range looked massive and though its peak extended way above the ceiling of the Gemini I was glad I had found it in clearer weather and had not blundered into it in the murk.

With renewed confidence I worked out a new course and as the western shore of Lake Victoria came into view we all shouted together. Shortly afterwards the aerodrome appeared on the water's edge to the north, but before landing we circled the clean, attractive and colourful town of Kampala in order to let our friends know that we had arrived safely. Despite being dead tired, sticky, crumpled and dirty we were almost deliriously happy. We had been in the air nearly seven hours since leaving Stanleyville, but nothing mattered so long as were alive and together.

On landing we enjoyed a luxurious rest in a modern hotel in Kampala. After a hot bath and a very satisfying, if not exactly sumptuous, meal we felt on top of the world. In the morning Wing Commander Kenneth Burns and his wife Muriel, the latter an old friend of Barbara's, were waiting for us in the hotel lobby ready to take us through the interesting parts of the town and country on the way to their home. I had always liked Kampala; it was an old town very much modernised with the British pattern of behaviour and administration clearly stamped upon it. In fact there was an amusing degree of Victorian protocol amongst the numerous British civil servants and busy executives, all enjoying life to the full. The shrewd and industrious Asiatics, whose stalls and bazaars flooded the streets wherever we went, as usual dominated ordinary commerce.

I had hoped to sell a Gemini to the firm for whom Kenneth Burns worked, but here I had my first setback on the sales tour. Kenneth had previously flown the Gemini and, after much consideration, had decided upon an all-metal American Beech Bonanza, which was due to arrive shortly.

Feeling clean and well rested we prepared for our flight from the Equator homewards to Johannesburg. On seeing the Gemini for the first time since our landing at Stanleyville I was shocked at the state of it. The water had been still pouring from it as we pegged it down for the night, but otherwise it did not look in bad shape. Now, in daylight, the burning sun had dried it out and the plywood skin had contracted between the ribs and given the aircraft a quilted appearance, though to the inexperienced the aircraft probably appeared normal. Barbara and I glanced at each other but said nothing as the Burns helped us with the luggage. I whispered to her that I would carry out an inspection of the aircraft at the end of the runway. A careful examination revealed nothing serious, though some of the distortions were more than an inch in depth; as far as I could see there were no glue failures. I told Barbara that we would take off carefully but if I were not happy we would land straight away. However, the little machine took off smoothly and settled down to normal cruising speed and, but for the port wing flying low, was normal in all respects.

We headed now on a south-westerly course, over the numerous emerald-coloured dots of islands that formed that part of Lake Victoria. Lake Edward, a short distance away, was our first check upon the accuracy of our track. We would then turn south for the regions of the Ruandi Urundi, something I had wanted to do all my life. As a child I had been brought up upon the tales written by the romantic authors of the time, who had used the fascinating, inaccessible and almost unknown region of darkest Africa as the theme for stories such as *The Queen of Sheba*. It was also, of course, the location of the greatest wealth in the world – King Solomon's Mine. This inhospitable area is protected by the vast expanse of water from Lake Victoria on the eastern side and the formidable forests and jungles of the Congo on the west. Dividing the two was a terrifying mountain range nearly 15,000 feet in height. During several previous attempts I had made to this magnetic spot there had always been heavy forbidding cloud cover in the upper regions of the mountains. On the lower slopes a wet clingy mist threatened any intrepid aviator foolish enough to try his luck. This time I had made out only a provisional flight plan and I was quite certain that we would have to fly south via the normal route of Nairobi and Tabora. Today, however, the weather was perfect and I welcomed the opportunity to visit the mysterious Lake Kivu high in the mountains; this, reputedly, was ice-blue in colour and, because of the mineral content, crystal-clear and free of both snakes and crocodiles. I also wanted to visit those tall, dignified members of the Watusi tribe.

It all lived up to our expectations and my only regret was that Alex was so young that the immensity of the unique experience was lost upon him. At Costermansville I thought of Livingstone and Stanley and the effort, pain and anguish of others to determine the source of the River Nile. I imagined too the contentious arguments that would have prevailed had they been told to forget about Lakes Albert and Victoria and been shown that the source of this mighty river from a small trickle was in fact but a short distance from where we stood.

When we flew low over Bukavu and followed a steep narrow cleft that disgorged enormous volumes of water from Lake Kivu into its large sister Lake Tanganyika, another facet of this intriguing continent gave me food for thought. I had been to many countries where geographical interest is taken in the Great Divide, where a ridge of very high ground causes the water, accumulating as rain, to run one way or another. The area over which we were now flying gave clear indication that, not only did this vast volume of water flow over the Equator to the Mediterranean thousands of miles away through the historic Nile, but from the same source flowed the mighty Zambesi on its way to the Indian Ocean, and also its even mightier twin, the Congo, winding almost unseen to the Atlantic. The knowledge that these three giant rivers flowed north, east and west from this spot absorbed me in deep thought and I could think of no other country that featured a phenomenon of such magnitude.

Alex's shouting roused me from my contemplation. He was pointing down excitedly to the huge herds of hippopotamus congregating in the shallow water on the east shore of Lake Tanganyika. A large family of elephants sprayed water through their swinging trunks onto their calves as they huddled for protection, peering up at us at the sound of our engines. The lake was alive with animals of every description. Unlike most other lakes there was no sign of any canoes, fishermen or habitation of any sort. As we passed low over the clear shoreline the most enormous crocodiles I had ever seen lumbered from their basking places in the hot sun and slipped into the shelter of deep water. And so it continued for hundreds of miles until, about midway, we came upon the first signs of human occupation, near the township of Albertville where we intended stopping for the night.

Albertville did little more than provide us with a straw mattress for a bed and a meal that merely staved off our hunger. The place itself was dull and uninteresting and I took the opportunity to work on the Gemini's airframe and engines. To my surprise the machine had suffered far less than I had at first anticipated. In the high humidity out of the scorching sun it appeared less distorted and wrinkled than it had first appeared in the morning light at Entebbe.

We set course for Ndola in Northern Rhodesia in good spirits. As we were flying over familiar ground and in light-hearted mood I gave Alex the controls in order to let Barbara rest in the back seat. I had shown him how to tweak the stick forward gently in order to wake Barbara from sleeping. When she complained he said cheekily: "Well, Mummy, if you don't like me flying, why don't you stay at home?"

**Right,** *Albert Fischer keeps an eye on young Alex as he sits on the wing of Miles Messenger OO-CCM at Moanda in July 1947. Formerly G-AGUW, this Messenger was flown from Woodley to Germiston by the author in March the previous year and delivered to Fischer in August.* (Author).

**Below,** *Albert Fischer's Messenger OO-CCM and Miles Gemini ZS-BRV at Moanda in July 1947.* (Author).

**Below,** *the Henshaws with Kenneth and Muriel Burns at Kampala the day after their eventful flight from Stanleyville on July 12, 1947.* (Author).

**Left,** *one last look at the Victoria Falls from Miles Gemini ZS-BRV before setting course for Pietersburg on July 15, 1947.* (Author).

**Below,** *this photograph of the Victoria Falls was taken from a BOAC Handley Page Halton in 1948.* (The Aeroplane photograph).

# Log of family tour around Africa, June 27th–July 15th 1947 in Miles Gemini ZS-BRV

| Date | From | To | Time | | Remarks |
|------|------|-----|------|---|---------|
| June 27 | Germiston | Pietersburg | 1 | 34 | |
| " | Pietersburg | Salisbury | 3 | 46 | |
| June 28 | Salisbury | Local flying | 1 | 15 | Demonstration |
| June 29 | Salisbury | Lusaka | 2 | 00 | |
| " | Lusaka | Local flying | | 20 | Demonstration |
| " | Lusaka | Elisabethville | 2 | 20 | |
| June 30 | Elisabethville | Kasambo | 1 | 20 | Port engine failure |
| " | Kasambo | Elisabethville | 1 | 20 | |
| June 31 | Elisabethville | Local flying | 1 | 30 | |
| July 1 | Elisabethville | Local flying | | 30 | |
| July 2 | Elisabethville | Vila Luso | 4 | 39 | Vapour locks |
| " | Vila Luso | Benguela | 3 | 03 | |
| July 3 | Benguela | Local flying | 2 | 00 | |
| " | Benguela | Luanda | 2 | 18 | |
| July 3 | Luanda | Local flying | | 45 | |
| July 4 | Luanda | Moanda | 2 | 15 | |
| July 5 | Moanda | Banana | 1 | 15 | |
| July 6 | Banana | Tshela | 2 | 00 | With Albert Fischer |
| " | Tshela | Moanda | | 40 | Jungle strip |
| July 7 | Moanda | Tshela | | 40 | |
| " | Tshela | Local flying | | 20 | |
| " | Tschela | Leopoldville | 1 | 20 | |
| July 8 | Leopoldville | Local flying | | 45 | Carb trouble, port engine |
| July 9 | Leopoldville | Kolo | 1 | 00 | With Barbara, Alex, van L |
| " | Kolo | Local flying | | 20 | |
| " | Kolo | Leopoldville | 1 | 00 | |
| " | Leopoldville | Local flying | 1 | 15 | |
| July 10 | Leopoldville | Banningville | 1 | 23 | |
| " | Banningville | Inongo | | 58 | |
| " | Inongo | Coquilhatville | 1 | 13 | |
| " | Coquilhatville | Lisala | 2 | 16 | |
| " | Lisala | Basoko | 1 | 23 | |
| " | Basoko | Stanleyville | 1 | 14 | |
| July 11 | Stanleyville | Local flying | | 20 | |
| " | Stanleyville | Kampala | 6 | 26 | |
| July 12 | Kampala | Lake Albert | 1 | 15 | |

| | | | | | |
|---|---|---|---|---|---|
| " | Lake Albert | Lake Kivu | 1 | 15 | |
| " | Lake Kivu | Costermans-ville | 1 | 00 | |
| " | Costermansville | Albertville | 2 | 32 | |
| July 13 | Albertville | Ndola | 4 | 42 | Flare path put out |
| " | Ndola | Livingstone | ? | | |
| July 14 | Livingstone | Local flying | 1 | 30 | |
| July 15 | Livingstone | Pietersburg | 4 | 56 | |
| " | Pietersburg | Germiston | 2 | 01 | Landed on schedule |

# CHAPTER 9

# BY THE GRACE OF GOD

My first meeting with Sir George Albu and other members of the board on my return at the General Mining office was to acclaim the success of our sales tour. Though my order book for the Gemini looked reassuring, I made the point that such orders were of no earthly use unless we could fulfil them. Since that hopeful day in March 1946, when I had landed the first postwar British flagship of the light aircraft industry, I had now reached some disturbing conclusions which, out of loyalty to the company, I did not voice beyond my own family. For a start I realised that although we had equipped our medium-sized workshops in a modest way, kept our stocks of materials and spares within reasonable limits and employed the best team of aeronautical engineers and mechanics, we were still not showing a profit.

I ran the administration in the same way as if it had been my own organisation. I gave concentrated thought, time and energy to every field in which we participated but I have to confess that my own commercial instincts were often influenced by other factors over which I had no control. The aircraft servicing establishment I had established on the Rand Airport was based on the premise that we should be regularly supplied, once production lines came into operation, by a substantial variety of new aircraft from the Miles factory at Woodley. I was aware that the Messenger was not, in itself, a viable commercial undertaking. However, combined with the attractive twin-engined Gemini, the small freight-carrying Aerovan and the metal four-engined Marathon airliner in full production, this would be a sound basis on which to develop a modern concept of aircraft maintenance and servicing as yet unknown in the Union. Furthermore, we had total franchise rights for the sale of Miles aircraft and many other products throughout Africa, so the overall potential looked promising.

But of course we never really got off the ground. I soon found not only a distinct prejudice against wooden aircraft but, in some instances, against British goods of any sort. This no doubt emanated from the experience of buying British cars. Heavier and larger American cars, unlike their British counterparts, were designed to withstand the rigours of the rough, corrugated gravel, sand and stone roads over which cars in that country were expected to travel many thousands of miles, day after day.

But the most important factor of all concerned delivery dates. I was mostly well received wherever I travelled and often welcomed by friends who, out of loyalty and patriotism to the old country, would waive all doubts to one side and be willing to purchase on the spot. Then, when I could only give a vague delivery date of some twelve to eighteen months, their fervour evaporated. Taking a long-term point of view, though my confidence in British aircraft design was paramount and I was certain we

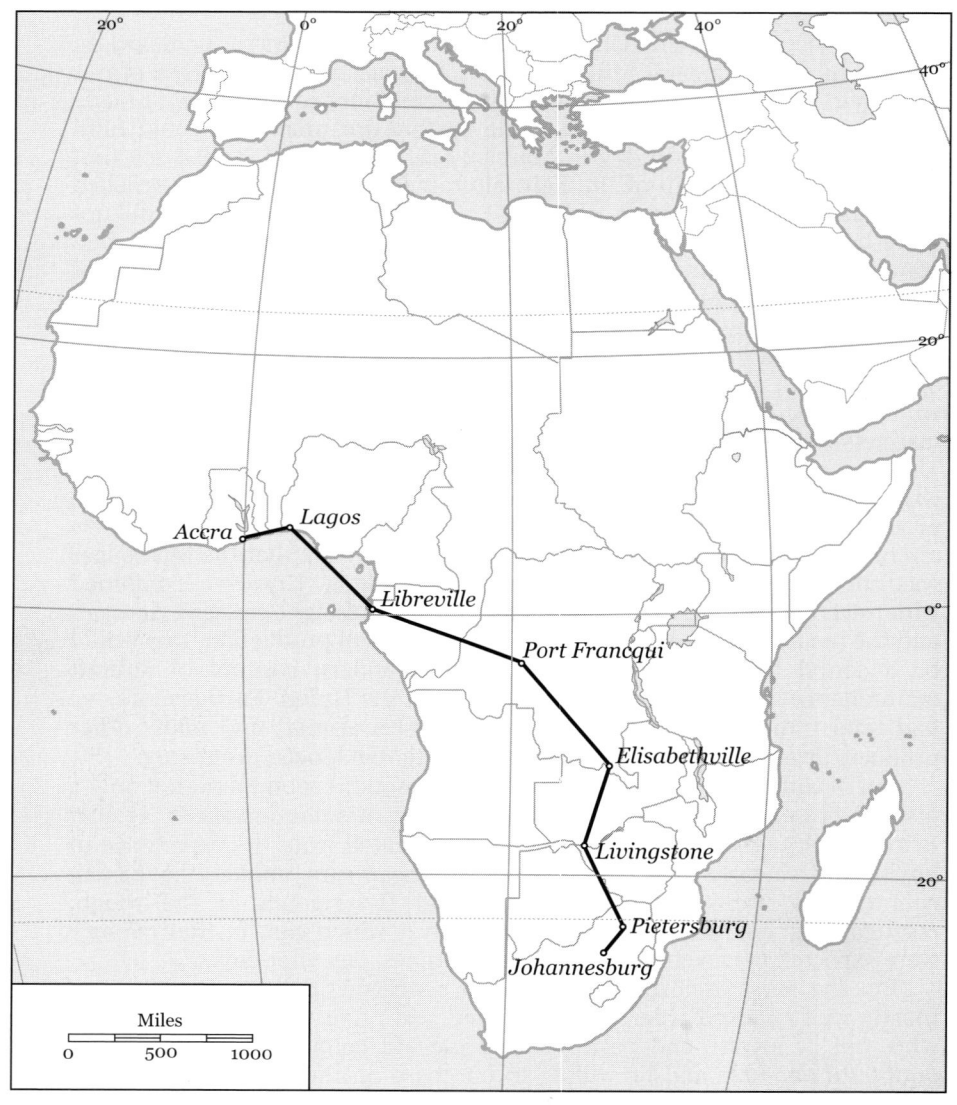

The author's route from Accra to Johannesburg,
flown in DH. 104 Dove ZS-AVH in August 1947.

could lead the world in this field, I was frustrated and perplexed by the Miles Aircraft Company's stubborn adherence to constructing all-wooden aircraft for export to tropical regions where maintenance and protection from the elements was minimal. I doubt many could know better than I the problems of operating small aircraft outside Europe. I was at the same time sympathetic to the manufacturers' difficulties during those early postwar years, when a skilled workforce and well-equipped shadow factories were geared only for the production of wooden aircraft. However, as I flew from one country to another, it was clearly evident that the writing was on the wall. The Americans were now building and selling a wide variety of light aircraft and although they could not outperform us, everyone with experience knew the American aircraft would still be flying when ours were heaps of borer dust on the sun-baked earth. The Americans were also able to give earlier delivery dates and prices I could not touch.

Left to my own devices I might have taken a stronger line, or operated in a somewhat different manner, but in all honesty I am not sure. There was always so much activity and my own work load was considerable, particularly after a long spell away from the office. There was a great deal of enthusiasm for the multitude of projects in hand, chiefly from Robbie, and I could easily have been blinded to the more realistic viewpoint that might otherwise have prevailed.

I had been fortunate in gathering together a good team that was staunchly loyal. Naturally enough some of the men were recruited from former Service personnel. I had only recently taken on a Major Alexander from a parachute regiment, whom I immediately liked, and David Haysom, the youngest Group Captain in the RAF. In order to get closer to the job I had an office on the airport in addition to the one I shared in Main Street, Johannesburg, with a most capable secretary in each.

About this time General Mining & Finance Corporation negotiated a merger with Anglo-Vaal Ltd. It was really a friendly association to fit into the group a small charter company that had been started by a former RAF pilot, Tommy Mitchell. For its size and capital it was profitable and the deal made good sense. We also became involved with another, larger, airline based near Pretoria which had run into financial difficulties. It became my task to find suitable land for our requirement to operate the entire group as an airfield and servicing centre, which would alleviate some of the excessive overheads involved with city municipalities.

It was just as well that I was totally absorbed in my work and family, as it took my mind off silly little irritating and unavoidable side issues. I tried hard to keep an open mind on the apartheid system and found myself swaying from one side to the other. I burned with the injustice, not when a white man was given a job that a Negro could not carry out but, so often, when promotion was in the offing, a stupid Afrikaner could take the post from an outstanding coloured man who was superior in every way. During the odd times I was called upon to collect Alex from his preparatory school I would hear his prissy little school friends determining the social status of their parents by whether or not they were collected by a glistening Cadillac with a white or black driver. I recall the rage I felt when returning to my car – after leaving it in a main street to make a short business call – to find that all the hub caps and embellishments had been removed. Invariably they had been taken and used to adorn the gaudy bicycles, often used by the natives, that already boasted half a dozen horns and as many mirrors and any other shiny item that could be added to the machine. I recall too the frustrating morning drive to the office. Every day, because of the impatience, aggressiveness and sheer bad driving of other motorists, there were hold-ups at the large roundabout linking four wide, well-built highways, followed by the long wait as the police came to sort out the tangled mess. The appalling amount of crime was so close at all times and there was the constant fear for the safety of one's family. And then there was the matter of the utter subjugation of thousands of wretched blacks, with their hordes of children, at the mercy of the will of the white man who knew that these people lived often in conditions unfit even for animals. I did not profess to know the answer to this problem, but I did feel that the South African Government was sitting on a time bomb with a smouldering fuse and needed quickly to come to grips with the reality of the situation.

With Ian Hay, David Haysom and the chief commercial Dakota captains Haroff and Boyd, we now had a number of competent pilots in the company and my own involvement in the flying aspect should have diminished, leaving me more time in the office. It did not, however, work out this way; I still carried out all the demonstration flying and more often than not would be asked by Sir George, Robbie, or other members of the board, to fly them to remote parts of Africa when the schedule was tight and demanding. I could have side-stepped some of these often tiring and sometimes difficult flights, but I was conscious of the compliment I was being paid and I would be the first to admit that I loved the freedom and adventure that such expeditions provided. At the same time, with each flight I sensed the inevitable change that was slowly controlling a way of life I had known since a boy – flying in Africa had given me a free rein.

With our first merger we had acquired one of the new de Havilland DH.104 Doves, ZS-AVH, an all-metal twin-engined aircraft that could be used as a small feeder airliner or as a luxury executive machine. Larger than the Gemini, it was also faster and more comfortable and I normally chose the Dove for expeditions that extended outside the Transvaal. It was on such a flight that I so nearly left the Dove to rot in the depths of the Congo jungle.

The mining divisions of our organisation were interested in a gigantic scheme to develop the wealthy deposits of bauxite in the Gold Coast, which entailed damming the Volta river upstream from Accra. I agreed to make the flight to Accra, taking Dr Hearne, St. John Bird and Col. Robbins. Because few servicing facilities would be available I thought it prudent also to take a flight engineer.

Leaving Germiston on August 4th 1947 the flight was uneventful, with the familiar weather patches around Luluabourg and the torrential storms from the Cameroons to Port Harcourt. My passengers were slightly less cheerful than they had been at the start of the flight, but I had warned them that if we were to adhere to the agreed schedule the journey would not be a picnic for anyone. There were no problems and we arrived at Accra on August 7th.

My problems really started on my return flight when landing at Lagos. I had arranged to spend the night there with a take-off planned for 2.30 am, but when I told the flying control officer, a young ex-RAF man in his first civilian job, he was adamant that, because the airfield was not equipped for night-flying, we would have to delay our departure until first light. I explained that we were equipped with landing lights and that in Africa it was quite normal for a pilot to use these aids when it was rare to find an airfield with night-flying facilities. This started quite a rumpus but, because I had never before been to Port Francqui and did not relish arriving late in the day without accurate reports and some information on the size and state of the airport, I dug in my heels. We argued for some time and in the end we compromised for a departure time of no later than 4 am. The control officer assured us that he personally would be on hand to give us official clearance.

After a short but restful sleep we took a taxi that dropped us off close to the Dove. In the sultry blackness of a tropical night we started preparations for the day ahead, there being no sign of the control officer. As four o'clock showed on the luminous dial in the well-equipped cockpit I asked Doug Mayel, the flight engineer, to start both engines. The new de Havilland Gipsy Queen engines were not always easy to start and by the time they were warmed up and we were ready for take-off it was well past our departure deadline. I once more walked over to the control office in case someone had arrived without our knowledge, only to find it unlit and locked. Cursing inwardly, I climbed back into the Dove and, telling my passengers that we would have to leave without official clearance, switched on the aircraft's landing light and in minutes we were on our way for our intermediary stop at Libreville.

After refuelling at Libreville I checked my flight plan and realised our schedule to Port Francqui was going to be tight. Had there been somewhere to eat and sleep at Libreville we would have opted for an overnight stay, but the place had not changed in years and was just as uninviting, in every sense of the word. The weather was now very good and after I had picked out one or two obvious features below that reassuringly matched with the map I felt my navigation was accurate. Twenty minutes before we were due to arrive at Port Francqui I spotted an isolated airstrip, just north of the bank of the River Kasai, which was not shown on my map. The sun was now low on the horizon so I marked the position of the strip carefully in pencil just in case I needed to land some other time in an emergency. I was not very concerned about finding Port Francqui as the River Kasai split at the point marked on the map and made its position most obvious. Suddenly Doug Mayel pointed through the forward window and there, spot on the nose, was the junction of the two rivers where they flowed into the main stream.

A glance at my watch indicated we were exactly on time, for which I was very pleased. By now daylight was diminishing rapidly as the sun sank below the horizon in a red glow. My contentment was short-lived as I peered in vain at the spot shown on the map to see no sign of habitation, or indeed any sign of life whatsoever. I looked askance at Doug Mayel, who was as puzzled as I. In the tropics the light goes down quickly and I cursed Lagos and the flying control officer for the mess in which we now found ourselves. I flew a wider circuit over the point where Port Francqui should have been, but in the dim twilight I could see nothing. I was now in serious trouble and a decision had to be made. Although the numerous sand bars on the River Kasai showed up fairly well in the fading light, the dense vegetation on either side had become a featureless mass.

My first reaction was to return and land on the emergency strip that I had so carefully marked on the map, but this was easier said than done. If I flew back along the river with the Dove's landing light switched on this would merely illuminate very clearly the slow-flowing water, the long narrow sand-banks and the splashes of scurrying crocodiles. Because the emergency strip was a few hundred yards away from the river in the jungle it could not be picked out with the light directly over the river. Even if I calculated my time accurately, the chances of finding the strip by weaving the aircraft in order to illuminate it with the light were remote indeed. Alternatively, if I flew over the jungle some little distance from the river on the side the strip was situated in the hope of locating it, the guiding reflection from the sandbars would be lost in the black background of dense undergrowth and I should be quickly lost.

Probably for the first time in my life I found myself in a precarious situation, not alone, but with trusting passengers who were unaware of the awful consequences now facing us. I could not see the faces of my passengers because I had purposely switched off all cabin and cockpit lights. I turned towards the cabin, and as I did so Dr Hearne anxiously came forward; I told him, more casually and calmer than I felt, that Port Francqui was not on the map as marked, but we hoped to find it by searching over a wider radius.

I had now to face the inevitable and decide where the aircraft was to be put down, probably for the last time. I was quite sure that I could land wheels-up on one of the numerous sandbars without damage to myself or the passengers, but the river was wide and we were in a remote part deep inside the Congo jungle. During the entire flight from Libreville I had not seen a single native canoe on the river. If by good chance I carried out a safe landing, and we were unhurt, we would then be faced with the formidable task of scrambling from the Dove's cabin and making our way over soft sand to the water's edge. If crocodiles did not intercept us we would have to swim an unknown distance to the nearest bank. Assuming that we could all swim reasonably well and that we avoided hungry predators and reached land, this would be only the beginning of our ordeal. The jungle extended right down to the water's edge on both sides of the river and its tangled undergrowth was impenetrable except for the small muddy gaps worn by crocodiles and other animals seeking access to drink and feed. For us to have struggled along the edge of the muddy bank miles from anywhere, with the almost certain prospect of falling victim to hungry jaws, was something I refused to contemplate, and I quickly pushed it from my mind.

Alternatively, I could put the Dove down on the trees near where I thought Port Francqui should have been, and hope that we might survive the crash. What I had seen from the air showed dense jungle devoid of clearings of any sort. Assuming we could climb unhurt from the wrecked machine, I knew that we would never be able to force a way through such a mass of twisted foliage, and there was every likelihood that we would end our days only yards from where we had started.

As I mulled over these thoughts I reached an almost desperate conclusion. If the worst did happen I would choose a sand bank nearest Port Francqui as indicated on the map and put down. If we were fortunate enough to slither on to the soft sand without the nose digging in and wrecking us all, I would then keep the doors of the aircraft closed in the hope that someone would have heard our engines in the dark and find us by the light of day. My assessment of the situation was immediately upset when I recalled the flash floods that were a constant feature in that wild and unfettered land. The wide river bed, with its narrow channels of water scattered here and there with clear sandy islands, could in a matter of minutes be transformed into a raging torrent carrying rocks, tree-trunks and other debris for hundreds of miles.

I was as bitter and angry with myself as I was with the flying control officer whose attitude had enforced the unnecessary delay back at Lagos. Of one thing I was confident, my navigation was not at fault. Port Francqui was obviously incorrectly marked on the map. The big question I now had to ask myself was where to search. The sun had long since gone and with it the horizon. The jungle below had now disappeared and merged into the sky as a black mass. There was nothing below but the dull snaking outline of this tributary from the Kasai, on which the map showed Port Franqui to be located, clearly defined by the lighter colour of the sand islands. I decided to use the confluence of the Kasai and the tributary as an accurate point of orientation from which I could make a series of ever-increasing turning circles. I did this out of despair; the fuel gauges were now reading uncomfortably low and I felt I should prepare my passengers for the worst. As I turned and switched on the cabin light I saw from their tense white faces that they were all tightly strapped in their seats and been assessing the situation between themselves. Dr Hearne looked at me expectantly and another had his eyes firmly closed and appeared to be mouthing a prayer.

Before I could speak, however, Doug Mayel, who until that moment had hardly spoken, touched me and said excitedly: "It may be nothing but I caught a glimpse of a fire over there." I looked in the direction he indicated, which appeared to be further along the river than we had previously searched. With nothing to lose I quickly turned the Dove to have a closer look.

In minutes we were circling, not a fire, but what appeared to be an electric or gas lamp apparently attached to the corner of a building. As we looked more closely we thought we could discern the outlines of a small European group of dwellings. I could see no movement but I was sure there was habitation below us and that we were looking down upon some kind of road or track. Reducing power on both engines, I partially lowered the flaps, switched on the landing light and began circling the light we had at first taken to be a fire. Our lights were surprisingly effective against the black background and on our first turn both Mayel and I thought we had seen a narrow gap of some sort just as the fading light cut across some tall trees. But, owing to the shadows cast, it was impossible to be sure. I made another circuit, this time a little wider, so that the interception at that point would run us down the gap instead of across it. The bright beam of our landing light shone between the trees this time and revealed what appeared to be a grass clearing with a red or rusty tin hut at one end. I made another dummy run the full length of the airstrip, for this I was now quite sure it was, and then lowered the undercarriage. I made a 360-degree turn, lowered the flaps fully and with as careful an approach as my new-found exhilaration would permit, set the Dove for a touchdown, the landing light providing a clear view over the long narrow gap with the shed discernible at the far end. We touched down smoothly on a level grass surface. Pulling up near the tin shed I closed the engines with a sigh of relief that said far more than any words.

For a moment there was dead silence. In the warm glow of the cabin lights we could now see each other clearly for the first time since the start of the drama. Suddenly the tension broke and everyone began talking and shouting at the same time. The cockpit was crushed and crowded as my trusting passengers came as one to slap me on the back in praise. My subdued response was, I think, taken as signs of strain. Had they known what I really felt they might well have reacted quite differently. Praise

A.V. Air Transport's DH.104 Dove ZS-AVH, flown by the author and so nearly left to rot in the depths of the Congo jungle. (Author).

**Above,** *an A.V. Air Transport DC-3 Dakota with three Miles Geminis (G-AJTF, G-AJTI and ZS-BRV) at Germiston, Johannesburg, awaiting delivery to customers in the Congo.* (Author).

**Below,** *leaving Accra for Lagos in DH.104 Dove ZS-AVH on August 12, 1947.* (Author).

**Below,** *DH.104 Dove ZS-AVH being prepared to leave the strip at Port Franqui in the early morning mist of August 14, 1947, the day after the near disastrous flight from Libreville.* (Author).

*"If crocodiles did not intercept us we would have to swim an unknown distance to the nearest bank"* (Painting of D.H.104 Dove ZS-AVH by Michael Turner).

was the last thing I wanted, or expected. In truth I was full of self-criticism and remorse. It was a very poor example of airmanship, whatever excuses might be made. There was only one person responsible and I had abused the loyalty and trust given by those who flew with me. But for the grace of God, at best I had almost lost a very nice aircraft, at worst I could have destroyed not only myself but all those entrusted to my care. Tired of waiting, and not knowing quite what to expect, we began unloading the personal luggage from the machine in the hope that someone would arrive in due course.

Suddenly we heard voices. A white man, wearing the minimum of bush gear, appeared out of the blackness speaking rapidly in French to a group of accompanying natives. He was a Belgian and did not appear unduly disturbed when I told him of our plight. Apparently the airstrip was rarely used, hence the long grass, and he refused to believe that there should have been any difficulty in finding it. With the aid of his flash-lamp I showed him my map and he was pleased to point out, with exasperating gestures, that Port Francqui was fifteen miles south-east of the spot indicated and that this tributary of the River Kasai was called the Lulua. Although much smaller in size it could in fact be followed all the way to that charming outpost where I had stayed with Barbara and Alex on their first flight across the Congo, Luluabourg.

**Jacques Lorentz (1910-1986)**
*During 1938-9 Lorentz was the South African representative of British Aviation Insurance Company Ltd. In 1940 he became Officer Commanding Flying at Navigation, Bombing & Gunnery Air Training Schools in Cape Town and East London. In 1942 he was made Senior Flight Commander of No 16. Squadron, South African Air Force (SAAF) and during 1943-5 he was the Commanding Officer of this squadron in North Africa and Italy. In 1945 Lorentz was seconded to the RAF as Officer in Charge of Accident Investigation in the Mediterranean Theatre. In 1946 he became South African representative of British Aviation Insurance Company and in 1950 joined the de Havilland Aircraft Company. In 1961 he was appointed Managing Director of Hawker Siddeley New Zealand, a position he held until his retirement in 1974.*

*An aerial view of Lympne aerodrome in Kent taken during the 1930s.*

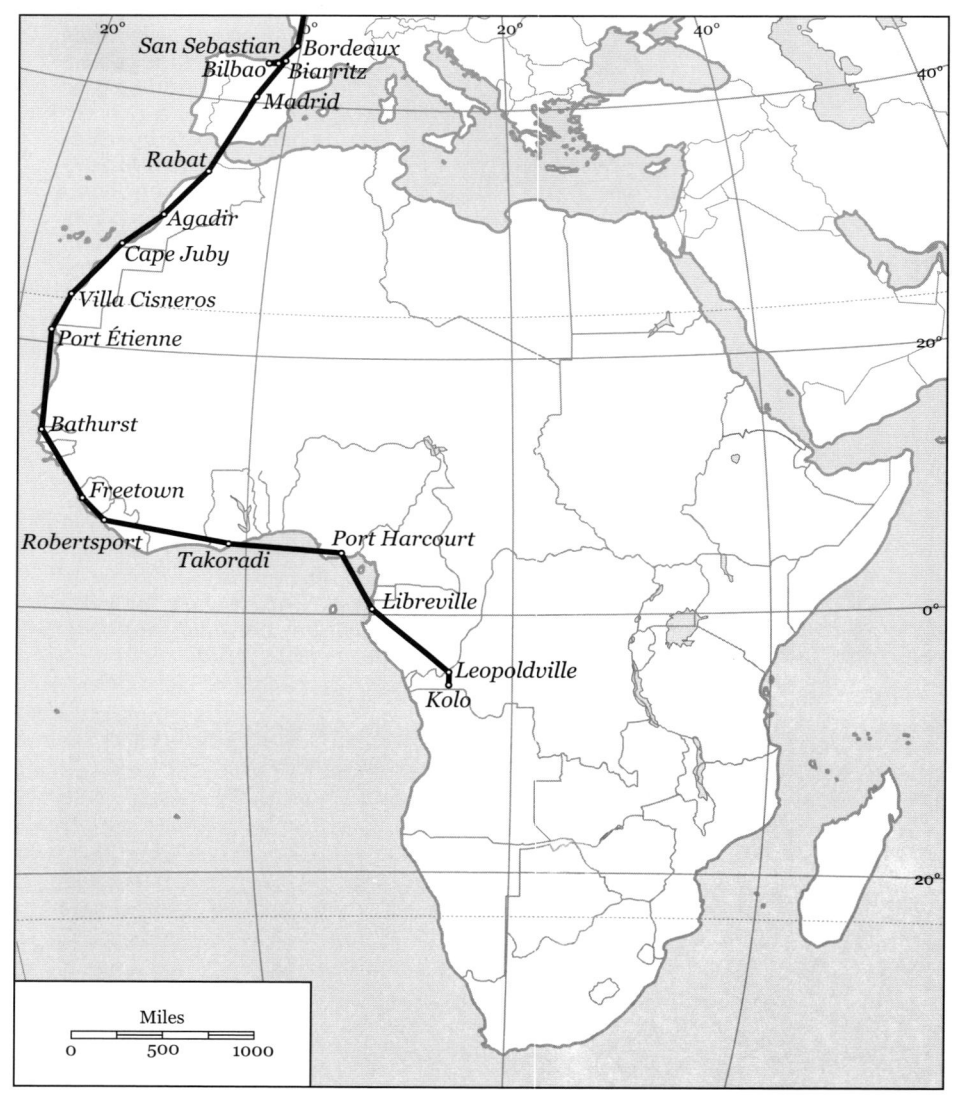

The author's route from Woodley to Leopoldville,
flown in Miles Gemini OO-CDP in January 1948.

# CHAPTER 10

## *ENTENTE CORDIALE*

On my return to Johannesburg there was consternation and gloom. During my absence Major Railing, Sir George Albu's top executive in the General Mining offices in London, had suddenly telephoned and asked if we had heard the rumours that the Miles Aircraft company was in serious financial difficulties. None of us believed a word of it, but further discreet telephone calls to London revealed that something most certainly was wrong. On November 13th 1947 my father had arrived to spend the winter away from the raw depressing gloom of England, and I had promised to take him with us by car for a tour of Zululand, Transkei and Cape Town. I had already told him that our intention was to return to Lincolnshire when my contract expired the next February, and he warned me that I would regret the decision. Apart from the postwar austerity, with rationing of clothes, food and fuel, we still had a socialist government with wasteful and time-consuming bureaucracy building up at an alarming rate. Administrative costs at all levels of government would increase overheads prohibitively before industry had a chance to create profits to pay for them.

I had also told George and Betty Albu that we would be returning home in the New Year; I felt very much a heel as I did so. I saw that Betty immediately understood, but I think George was irritated and incredulous.

"What more do you want?" he demanded. "We have everything anyone could desire out here, and you want to go back to Europe where there is nothing. The prospects and potential with us is unlimited for both you and your family, and I am sure you will regret it once you get back. I am not going to accept your resignation, you can take six months leave and let me know your answer at the end of it."

I thanked him and said how much I appreciated his friendship and the kindness he and his family had shown us, but it was just one of those things. I could not really explain it but I was quite sure that neither Barbara nor I could settle in South Africa. Robbie was, as always, easy to talk to and sympathetic to many of my points of view. Because we did not know at the time the serious situation arising in the Miles Company, he suggested that I might change my mind when aircraft production got fully under way. Ian, of course, as a close friend, knew my feelings and, strange to say, wished he could join us.

My decision made no difference to our working arrangements, but when the Miles bombshell did eventually explode we were about to arrange for the van Lancker Gemini to be delivered by another pilot. A formal board meeting was called and it was decided that, as I knew the Miles group better than the other two members, I should fly at once to the UK and report on the situation in so far as it affected our own interests. To save costs it was agreed that I should collect the Gemini, particularly as it had been paid for, and deliver it to Kolo, some hundred miles south of Leopoldville.

At this time we were running a regular passenger service to Croydon with Dakotas. Usually the aircraft were filled to capacity flying back to Africa but were empty on flights to the UK. I decided to go with Haroff and Boyd on their next flight to England.

An old friend, Colonel Jacques 'Jacko' Lorentz, head of British Aviation Insurance in South Africa, had business to conduct in the UK, and he asked if he could join me on the flight both ways. Jacko had served in the South African Air Force during the war and had a distinguished record as a fighter and bomber pilot. He became Managing Director of the de Havilland Aircraft Company (later Hawker Siddeley New Zealand) and later still worked as an aviation consultant.

We left Germiston in Dakota ZS-BCJ on December 27th 1947. During the outward flight we had plenty of room, so that we either read or slept most of the way. We arrived overhead Croydon on December 30th, where the weather was its normal winter gloom. In the awful murk we very nearly hit high ground and an accident was only averted by the swift action of the second pilot, who overruled the captain, and we diverted to Blackbushe.

I immediately pressed on to Woodley and was shocked and saddened by what I found. The once-thriving factory was now dark, cold and lifeless with unfinished aircraft spread around in a ghostly manner. Gone were the friendly faces I had known and liked for so many years. I was no longer able to enjoy discussions over a pleasant meal in a private dining room with Fred, George or Blossom Miles. When I entered what had once been Fred Miles' office a small, expressionless man, who acknowledged me without a smile, met me. He thawed a little when I introduced myself and he explained that, as Official Receiver, his job was to sell everything at the best price he could get. My meeting with him was a long one. Every aspect of our association was discussed in a correct, if rather frigid, manner. Knowing my history and past associations with the Miles company and its founder members I think he expected hostility, but at the same time realised that I could, through our South African company, capitalise many of the assets with which he had to deal on behalf of the creditors. Apart from the question of continuity with those products falling under our franchise rights I was also concerned that, having sold aircraft in good faith, the spares and technical back-up should be made available at the outset. It soon became clear that the Receiver could not give any guarantee on these matters at this stage; his main concern was to realise as much cash as he could for anything that could be taken away. I had to accept that he was a ruthless competent professional who knew his job. He also revelled in cutting out what he saw as so much dead wood in order to get to the heart of the problem.

During this somewhat traumatic period Miles had just completed the installation of de Havilland Gipsy Major 10s into the Gemini, replacing the lower-powered Cirrus Minors, but none had so far been sold. The Receiver asked me if I would fly this experimental Gemini, give my opinion of its qualities and make a bid for those that could be assembled. He said that stocks of Cirrus engines were depleted but the company had a number of Gipsy 10s in stock that could be turned into cash. The irony of the situation was that for some considerable time I had been urging Miles to fit the more powerful Gipsy engine in the Gemini, but they had refused for a number of reasons. I flew the Gipsy 10-engined Gemini for 45 minutes on January 4th 1948.

After seeing the Receiver I stayed that night at the Swan Hotel in Sonning, run by the brother-in-law of Ralph Robinson, who himself was the brother of Robbie (Albert Robinson). Ralph had been with the Miles Aircraft company for years and rose up through the firm to become a very senior executive, involved with much of the financial restructuring during its expansion, particularly during the negotiations for a proposed merger with Rolls-Royce. Ralph was not as home when I arrived but his mother-in-law, whom I knew, was soon in tears and bewailing the unhappy plight in which her poor daughter had been placed. I saw Ralph the following Sunday morning and we had a long chat over coffee at his delightful cottage. The demise of the Miles organisation was much more involved than I realised, and already the threats of long and costly litigation were being felt from various quarters. As I asked Ralph what the chances were of survival the bells of the local church rang out in what I thought was a sombre and depressing manner, reminding me of Hemingway's book *For Whom the Bell Tolls*. Robinson, reading my thoughts and nodding towards the sound, said: "Yes, that says it all."

I left Sonning saddened and disheartened, pondering the effects of this calamity on the British light aircraft industry as a whole. I had seen Fred and Blossom Miles build up from nothing a large aircraft company that had made its mark during the critical years of the war with production of its training aircraft for the Royal Air Force. I now saw it as the only British aircraft manufacturer likely to keep the country's talent for designing and producing aircraft for private flying to the forefront. I had flown all the wide variety of Miles types over a period of 16 years and I was conscious that the termination of this imaginative, ebullient and determined little group would have repercussions that would be felt in private and civil aviation for decades to come. Many prewar designers and producers of suitable light aircraft for the private owner had disappeared. Companies such as Avro, Blackburn, de Havilland and Percival had since turned their considerable resources to producing aircraft for more lucrative markets. As I mulled over the situation I reached the conclusion that the British light aircraft industry was now dead and the way was now left open for the Americans to step in.

During the next few days, with the short daylight hours of winter, I found myself under pressure to complete my tasks on time. I had felt duty bound to see as many Miles executives as was possible. Understandably most were keeping a low profile and could not easily be found. Others, such as Captain 'Bush' Bandidt, had in fact returned to Australia. It was also necessary to accumulate as many test flights on the Gemini OO-CDP as conditions would allow. I also had to select suitable spare parts to load on board for the long flight ahead. Because of the stringent flight control regulations in the Sudan, which had caused me so much trouble in the past, I had decided to use a little-used route to the Congo which, l was told, had no flying restrictions imposed upon it. Once I arrived at Leopoldville I had to connect with an airline flight back to Johannesburg. The schedule was therefore a tight one and if I missed the connection at Leopoldville it would certainly create problems.

I had arranged to meet Jacko at Lympne on January 6 and I flew there from Woodley in the new Gemini. On arrival I was pleased to see Jacko already waiting for me by the wooden customs sheds. We stayed the night at a small hotel on the boundary of the aerodrome in readiness for an early take-off the following morning. An old friend, Mrs Ann Attrey (formerly Mrs Davis) owned the hotel. She, with her first husband Eric and brother-in-law Duncan, had run the Brooklands and Lympne flying clubs and was responsible for organising some of the most celebrated and successful prewar international race meetings in the country. John Attrey made me feel very much at home although he regretted that Anne could not be present, as she was about to give birth to their first child. I was sorry to have missed her, as the last time we had met had been at one of those marvellous prewar Lympne events at which a tragic crash had killed her husband.

I well remembered the races. I was not only lucky enough to win the International Contest but Anne had searched the antique shops to find a beautiful pair of pewter mugs which she presented as a prize for the fastest time.

Jacko and I were eager to get away at first light in the morning. Our plans however seemed to collapse the moment we stepped from our warm and comfortable quarters. There was no light and the wet, cold fog sent a shiver down our backs. We planned to make Madrid and stay there for the night, and after filing our flight plan with the control officer, we cleared immigration and groped our way to the machine parked out on the grass. We filled in a little time by making a thorough inspection of the Gemini's airframe and engines, by which time it had got a little lighter. However, looking at the hangar a few yards away we realised how thick was the fog, and our spirits sank lower by the minute. As we peered at the rolling mist to the east we thought we perceived a very faint horizon at ground level. With little else to do we walked over the aerodrome, which fell away at a gradient

*"As we sped across the sandy airfield, with the sage bushes throwing ghostly shadows as we charged into them, we crouched low in the cockpit in expectation of what was to come."*
(Painting of Miles M.65 Gemini OO-CDP by Michael Turner).

Samuel R. Hogg, DSO, MC, FCA was Receiver and Manager of Miles Aircraft Ltd during 1947-48. After a long meeting with Hogg the author described him as a ruthless competent professional who knew his job. Hogg's task was to sell the Miles assets at the best price he could get. (Hay Wrightson Ltd - via Museum of Berkshire Aviation).

Halcyon days. The all too rare sight of a post-war British light aeroplane in quantity production! Miles Geminis on the line at Woodley aerodrome, Reading during the winter of 1946-7, shortly before the company collapsed. (via Philip Jarrett).

from where we were parked. After a few hundred yards, to our surprise, we saw the barbed wire boundary fence beyond which the ground showed quite clearly. We were actually beneath low cloud, and as we stood our heads were almost in it. Knowing the aerodrome well I thought we might as well taxi the Gemini down to this low point of the field and, using the fence as a fog-line, take off parallel to it. With Jacko walking ahead of the machine, we carefully taxied to the aerodrome boundary and turned as close to the fence as was prudent, with the nose pointing up the hill, which I knew would gave ample room for take off. I set the directional gyro due west and calculated we should have 150-200 yards before we were enveloped in the low cloudbank.

We were not quite airborne as we lost sight of the fence and we continued blind. As the wheels retracted I put the Gemini into a steep left-hand spiralling climb. Keeping over what I hoped was the aerodrome I remembered there were high steel masts nearby, but could not recall exactly where they were located. We broke cloud in clear conditions at a little less than 3,000 feet. Well above us was another layer of stratus but, to our delight and relief, the English Channel showed up clearly in the distance beyond the low cloud from where we had just climbed.

The flight to Madrid, directly over the Pyrenees, was a long leg and I did not relish trying to locate it in the dark. Our weather forecast had warned of strong south-westerly winds with heavy rain and snow over the mountains. At first we maintained our height and headed for the first land fix on the French coast. Jacko, who was navigating, said:, "I think we must be going backwards or else this slide-rule is playing tricks." When we had started the sea had appeared as a flat millpond; now, as we peered down, it was tossing around small boats near the shore as if they were corks. Dropping to a lower altitude we realised we were going to have a long, wet and rough ride and, worse still, we had no hope of reaching Madrid without refuelling. Tightly strapped into our seats we bucked our way into the teeth of the gale with a deluge of rain streaming over the windscreen. In an effort to gain a little more ground speed we sank lower. Through the side windows we had a good close-up view of the terrain which, not long previously, had been a bloody battlefield. Villages and towns lay silent and unoccupied, the recent ravages defined by heaps of rubble left untouched. As we flew further south the war damage became less obvious and the only diversion was an imaginary race with a car, almost hidden from view in a swirl of muddy spray, as it sped along one of the many straight roads.

After struggling for more than three hours Jacko suggested that as we could no longer reach Madrid, perhaps it would be wiser to refuel at Bordeaux before crossing the Pyrenees. We landed at Bordeaux after four and three quarter hours in the air. Before the flight we had agreed that Jacko would attend to all customs and immigration paperwork and that I would deal with flight plans, servicing and refuelling. This worked out very well and our clearance from Bordeaux gave us both cause for satisfaction.

However the Met. report soon dampened our spirits. Though the wind had now dropped the rain poured relentlessly over the windscreen as we departed from Bordeaux. I read the forecast that Jacko had handed to me and, as I expected, there was a heavy snowfall predicted over the mountains and the icing level was unusually low. After a brief discussion we agreed that it was best to make for Bilbao by keeping to the coast, and clearing all formalities in order to enable us to make an early morning start for Africa. Enormous seas were breaking over the rocky coast as we crossed the frontier. It gave us a very rough ride as we crept round the high outpoints but we were nevertheless confident of reaching our destination before darkness. The froth and foam streaming off the pounding waves made the light appear better than it really was and I felt very depressed as we turned over the dull dirty mass that was in fact Bilbao. The lights of the town accentuated the awful drabness of the streets. At first neither Jacko nor I were aware that we had found the airport. All we could see in the dull light and the rain was a partially open area on which construction equipment and drainpipes were haphazardly strewn everywhere. There appeared to be a small area that was clear but under the torrential rain it looked like a quagmire. I knew that even if I made a safe landing my chances of taking off again were small. Without any hesitation we decided to return to San Sebastian.

It was almost dark by the time we swung over the town and picked out the small airfield. As we flew a dummy run over it we both gasped when we saw how badly flooded it was. We now had no alternative other than to return and try and find the small landing ground at Biarritz. We knew this was not going to be easy; although the Gemini had a good central beam landing light fitted in the nose it was not much use for locating specific points. We made straight for the town of Biarritz; from previous visits made before the war I remembered that the landing ground was situated on a ridge that rose sharply from the built-up area on the seafront. We were lucky when Jacko quickly discerned a shadowy clearing on the ridge and as I switched on the landing light we could see that it was a field with quite long grass, but dry and level. On landing it took some time to find someone who would telephone the Shell agent for fuel. There was no sign of customs, immigration or the police. Living as I then was in South Africa it was easy to forget what the ravages of years of war had done to Europe. The population appeared still in a daze, confused and scarred, both mentally and physically.

The Shell agent eventually turned up in a shabby little car driven by a man in a dirty torn French Army uniform. We were taken to a tin shed in which was stored a modest amount of petrol stacked in four-gallon tins. In the most uncomfortable conditions imaginable we all began the laborious task of filling the Gemini's tanks. We first stuck a steel spike through the top of each tin before carrying them to the aircraft. With an old raincoat to keep off the rain, Jacko and I held the chamois leather funnel whilst we poured from the awkward tins, trying not to drench ourselves with the volatile fuel. With refuelling completed we asked in broken French if it was possible to obtain a taxi with which to find a hotel. At first we received a very negative response; the man in the shabby uniform, pointing to the petrol tins, indicated that he had no fuel of his own and that he had only driven to the field at the insistence of the Shell agent. With gestures and poor French we suggested that we would pay the man his fare and give him a four-gallon tin of petrol if he would take us to the town and then collect us at first light the next morning. The man's eyes brightened immediately and he willingly agreed. But the Shell agent, I thought, looked a little uncomfortable, probably not so much because of the dubious ethics but for the fact that if the gendarmes found coloured petrol in the car's tank awkward questions could well be asked. I reassured the agent by saying in front of the driver that the petrol would be locked overnight in the aircraft and would only be handed over when we left the following morning. That way the agent would not see the exchange of petrol and, as I murmured in an aside to Jacko, it would also ensure that the taxi driver turned up in the morning! We climbed aboard the dilapidated car and misfired our way to the Miramar, which I recalled as a renowned and high-quality hotel. There was no shortage of beds but the once-sumptuous reception rooms looked shabby and needed renovation. For our first meal of the day we dined alone.

The driver was on time the next morning as we carried our holdalls out on to the dimly-lit street. The rain had stopped at last and although it was overcast the weather was dry and cold. When we arrived at the airfield it was quiet and deserted. We lost no time in squaring our account with the driver, who thanked us profusely. After take-off the overcast hung heavily on the adjacent mountains and, with the possibility of icing, we turned seawards before commencing a slow tedious climbing turn which we hoped would bring us out into clear air. It was not long before ice began forming on the windscreen and side windows, making it impossible to keep an eye on the state of the wings. As we climbed so the performance of the engines gradually deteriorated, to the point where I decided I was going to have to abort the climb. Then suddenly there was brilliance all around us, and as we scraped the ice away from the small observation window we could see blue sky. Above and way over to the south-east we could see the ominous black-looking peaks of the highest mountains. It took ages for the ice to disperse and we slowly picked up our normal cruising speed. After passing Madrid we calculated our ETA for Agadir and worked out that we would have to put down in Rabat for more fuel. As we headed contentedly into Africa in the brilliant sunshine and perfect azure sky, the Straits and Rock of Gibraltar looked like a holiday postcard.

The aerodrome at Rabat buzzed with activity and for the first time we saw evidence of the French Air Force, amidst a variety of British and American fighters and bombers parked haphazardly around the aerodrome perimeter. Leaving Jacko to clear the formalities I taxied up to the fuel base, adjacent to a strong high wire and steel fence. Pressed so close against the wire that it bulged in places were hordes of scruffy-looking men dressed in an incredible variety of dirty, torn and ill-fitting garments. One quite good-looking man pleaded with me through the wire. I gathered that he had been wrongly imprisoned and he asked if I could give a message to an important personage in Paris. Knowing the problems with some of the Vichy French, and the danger in which I could put us if we were seen fraternising, I pretended not to hear. The man looked so sincere and sad that for a while afterwards my conscience pricked me as to whether or not I should have helped him.

Despite the tedious and dilatory behaviour of the French control officers we were able to take off in good time to arrive in Agadir well before sundown. We were surprised to observe that the airfield, although little used, was heavily garrisoned with barbed wire around the boundaries, and with machine gun emplacements at odd intervals around the perimeter. There was a small control tower but no sign of any aircraft. On landing Jacko walked over to the tower and I proceeded with the usual formalities. I was pleased to find that petrol and oil was quickly available and by the time I had completed a close inspection of the Gemini's airframe and engines there was still no sign of Jacko. After a while I decided to walk over and find out what was delaying him.

As I stepped into the small tower office I immediately sensed trouble. A portly officer with three gold bands on his sleeves, wearing a none too clean uniform, was talking loudly and aggressively to a French sergeant at a small untidy desk, while another officer listened intently. Before I could say a word Jacko interceded: "We have problems, Alex, we are not supposed to land here without prior permission, nor can we cross the desert unless our machine is equipped with radio – and they are not very friendly."

In an amenable manner I turned to the commandant and apologised for any infringement that we might have incurred. I also said that in London we had been told that, whilst there were stringent regulations covering flights across the Tanezrouf sector of the Sahara, no specific permission was required for a flight from Agadir to Villa Cisneros and Port Étienne. I said that we had advised Rabat control of our intention to land at Agadir and no objections had been raised, and that we were flying in a private non-radio aircraft. If the commandant refused to allow us to proceed it would necessitate flying back to Oran and then an enormous distance via Cairo, Khartoum, Elisabethville and finally Leopoldville. This would result in losing our airline connection and we would suffer costly and time-consuming delays as a result. This brought a snorted reply in broken

English that was certainly rude, if not offensive. Out of the corner of my eye I noticed a smirk of satisfaction on the face of the other officer. I asked if we could make an early start in the morning should we be compelled to return. In a pompous and patronising manner the commandant informed us that he would not allow us to leave until after 1000 hrs. Then, as if to put me in my place, he said that if I knew anything about flying in that part of Africa I would also know that fog grounded all aircraft until it was burnt off by the sun. After meekly accepting all he had to say I asked if we could at least refuel the aircraft and disperse it to a safe part of the airfield. To this he grudgingly acceded.

As we walked from the tower Jacko asked what the hell we were going to do next. I outlined what I had in mind and after he had recovered his composure he said: "I wish to God we could do what you plan, but you have forgotten one vital issue: I had to hand over the journey logbook to the control officer and he will not release it until it is time to for our departure." He gasped when I told him that whilst the 'fat frog' was berating us the others were so distracted they did not see me sneak the logbook from off the commandant's desk.

On our way in the fading light to the town of Agadir we took careful stock of the layout of the airfield. We noted the odd places where the barbed wire fence had rusted and so could be penetrated with ease. When we reached the hotel we were fortunate to find that the manager spoke very good English and was obviously pro-British. We asked if he would explain something to our Arab driver and if he thought he could be trusted. We explained that we wanted to be picked up at our hotel at 0100 hrs and then driven to the airfield. We told the driver he was to keep his lights dimmed and, because we did not want to disturb the airfield personnel at that time of night, he was to take us direct to where the aircraft was parked by the perimeter fence near the entrance road. We would pay double his normal fare and if he kept quiet and did a good job we would give him an additional bonus. This plan was relayed to the Arab who apparently had been a driver with the American Forces and spoke better English than we had at first thought. I suspected that he soon caught on to what we were about to do. Both Jacko and I felt that the Arab was enjoying the thought of participating in a clandestine operation that would put one over on the French.

Under the circumstances, and possibly due to the effects of a very good meal on empty stomachs, we both slept well that night. The manager had to knock hard on the door to awaken us at the appointed time. We had a cold shower, gulped some hot coffee and braced ourselves for what lay ahead. The Arab driver was as good as his word but we were surprised to note that he had brought a companion with him. We had not bargained for this and I whispered to Jacko: "If they don't drive direct to the airfield, you grab the passenger and I'll grab the driver."

The street in which the hotel was situated formed part of the central town, but it also led in the general direction of the road to the airfield. When we climbed into the decrepit Citroen we both memorised the brilliant star configuration in relation to the road and the position we reckoned the airfield to be. But as we crawled along in the dim light we lost sight of a particularly bright star that was acting as our guide and our spirits fell. There was an audible sigh of relief when we realised that we had passed under trees and that the canopy of leaves had temporarily obliterated the stars from our view.

We drove along in complete silence, poised for trouble. I had anticipated reaching the airfield much sooner and was about to get agitated when the driver slowed to less than walking pace. I jumped out of the car and although there was no moon I could see vaguely the rolled barrier of wire and the dull outline of buildings some distance ahead. It took some time to search along the fence and find the dark shadow that was the Gemini. Having ascertained that we had found the right gap I returned to the car and shook each man by the hand and gave them more than enough to have made the escapade worth their while. I instructed them not to rev the engine and asked them to keep their lights off until after we had left. All was dead quiet as we groped around, putting our bags into the Gemini. After checking as well as I could that nothing had been tampered with, I prepared the engines for starting.

Jacko, fretting as I made sure that everything was set to go, said: "I think I saw some movement by that first gun emplacement, the buggers will open up any minute now." In the warm North African air the port engine burst into life with an explosive roar, sounding far louder in the dark silence than it really was. As we sweated to get the starboard engine going we expected an immediate furore of activity from the gun pits and the control tower. I dared not use a light and in my nervous state my fingers seemed to be all thumbs. Just as the engine fired and the rev counter needle flew round the dial all hell was let loose. Lights came on near the hangars, the control became ablaze and we could see figures running about in all directions. Jacko called: "For Christ's sake, Alex, get a move on, they're about to let loose with everything they've got."

In order not to give our position away it was not possible to run the engines up to full power and it would thus take more time to warm them up. I was afraid of power failure taking off with the engines cold and in order to force self-discipline I 'spent a penny' near the open cockpit door, knowing it would take me a good minute or so. We kept ourselves in complete darkness and I do not think that the airfield guards could see much of us other than the dull flames from the engine exhausts. We could hear orders being shouted and could see shadowy forms rushing here and there, and we expected to be surrounded any second. Jacko shouted one final plea and I jumped into the cockpit, set the gyro-compass on the correct setting and opened up both engines. The moment the engines reached full power Jacko switched on the powerful nose landing light.

As we sped across the sandy airfield, with the sage bushes throwing ghostly shadows as we charged into them, we crouched low in the cockpit in expectation of what was to come. After a final bouncing and bucking we lifted into the air and there was a smoothness and relative silence as we sank back into our seats. After catching our breath Jacko and I shook hands. Below we could see the airfield lights around the main buildings with figures scurrying about like rabbits. The lights of Agadir showed up very clearly and we set course for Villa Cisneros. We hoped to get an accurate check of our ground speed and fuel consumption before proceeding to Port Étienne over 2,000 miles away.

At first we hummed along in the clear night, a faint streak of white surf visible along the shore below. Then, in customary manner, the fog started to form as the warm air of the desert mixed with the breeze off the cold Atlantic. After flying for hours on a direct compass course over a white carpet of cloud I realised we must have overshot Villa Cisneros, obscured by thick fog, and we were now committed to make Port Étienne. Jacko had reckoned that our ETA was six hours fifteen minutes from take off and that we would arrive in a quarter of an hour. The fog was still thick and obscured the desert for several miles inland, whilst to the west there was an unbroken blanket of pure white stratus. Just as we were debating whether or not we should throttle back and wait for the fog to clear, Jacko yelled out that he could see yellow sand below and then, ahead, a clump of solitary buildings appeared.

I can only describe Port Étienne as hell on earth. Alongside some wooden sheds was a level stretch of sand marked at each corner by some rough-painted stones. As we touched down two swarthy almost naked men walked over to us. At first I thought they were natives, as the sun had burned their skin until it was almost black. They were dirty and unshaven but friendly and helpful as they hacked into the four-gallon tins with complete abandon. We felt sorry for these men having to endure such appallingly hot and depressing conditions, but they soon made light of it. Their ration of 30 litres of water had to suffice for everything, from drinking to washing each day.

The heat and the brilliance of the blinding sun on the almost white sand, unbroken by the slightest vestige of vegetation or foliage, made our quick climb away from that cauldron a huge relief. As the Gemini climbed slowly into cooler regions we gasped for air. Our landing at Bathurst, by comparison, was like landing in the middle of Piccadilly Circus. It had a single magnificent tarmac runway, an abundance of shrubs and trees and a comfortable hotel with accommodation operated efficiently by British Overseas Airways. We had not eaten or drunk at our previous port of call and we now looked forward to our first meal since leaving Agadir.

Our take-off next morning was 0200 hrs. There was no problem and the control officer apologised for having to charge £1 for the use of the runway lights. The runway appeared enormous as the ground lights disappeared out of our view as we climbed into the night. We set course for Monrovia but I hoped to get a fix over Freetown after four-and-a-half hours' flying.

I had planned to fly at a height of 7,000 feet but as we climbed we both became aware of an intense blackness surrounding the aircraft. We could not see any part of the wings and straight ahead the windscreen was as black as ink. Although we were not in cloud there was not a glimmer of light, even the sky was devoid of stars. In the blackness the luminous compass and other instruments shone like beacons and somehow amplified the claustrophobic effect we both felt. It felt so eerie and uncomfortable that I climbed a further 1,000 feet, just to be on the safe side. What we did not realise at the time was that we had been flying through the *hamataan*, a wind that stirred up the sand and dust from the desert. On reaching more humid climates it deposited a dirty film over everything it touched. As a result we were almost cocooned in a thick dirty deposit that in the darkness of night had blacked out vision from the cockpit.

We never did see Freetown, but landed at Monrovia with the early morning mist and steam rising from the adjacent jungle. We were prevented from getting away quickly by a sleepy American NCO who was unable to supply fuel of the correct octane. The flight to Takoradi was tiring and uneventful but the confident feeling that we should now reach the Congo on schedule buoyed us up. It was then that our troubles began.

Jacko had to telephone Accra for permission for us to take off that night. The flying control was under the jurisdiction of a young Englishman who pompously informed Jacko that he would not countenance night flights in his region by us or anyone else. We then went over to the customs and immigration offices, recently taken over by Ghanaians following the British withdrawal from what had once been the Gold Coast. A 6ft 6in Negro dressed in a white uniform liberally decorated with gold braid confronted us. Saying nothing he gave us both a sheaf of forms and indicated in an imperious manner that they were to be completed in triplicate. We were tired, dirty and bleary-eyed but nevertheless sat down to complete the forms as best we could. Having wearily filled in all the questionnaires and signed each in triplicate the forms were handed over to the sullen officer. Almost without a glance he flung them back at us with more of the same forms, and barked that they had been completed incorrectly. Patiently we sat down once more and asked him what he expected of us. His attitude at once became truculent and abusive; he snatched the forms from Jacko and shouted that we could not leave his office until he was satisfied. Jacko, who had a great deal more experience with this kind of situation than I, blurted out authoritatively: "You've been drinking, I can smell Palm brandy on your breath."

At this the huge man rose and struck out wildly at Jacko, shouting, "You white pigs, I spit on you. We are in power now, you will do as we say." Jacko had sprung out of reach of the man's swinging arms and I looked around for something solid with which to knock him out. Opening the door I was about to shout for another officer to aid us when a small but seemingly hostile crowd that had been attracted by the noise confronted me; they appeared to be field workers and they carried spades, scythes, machetes or heavy wood staves.

We quickly realised our predicament. I saw that a few yards away our car was waiting and that the driver was beckoning vigorously for us to join him. Remembering the old adage *'he who runs away lives to fight another day,'* I shouted to Jacko to jump into the car. He did so but not before the huge Negro had taken a lunge at me, spitting curses as he did so. Though he missed my face he caught me painfully on the nose, but by the time he and the bewildered mob had realised what we were doing we were in the car and away. We tried that night to put our complaint to the most senior official and although we received sympathetic consideration we were told very firmly that there was nothing the British Government could do about the incident.

Low cloud and mist faced us the next morning and neither of us relished the long flight over the Bights of Benin and Biafra to Libreville. Because of the ugly incident the previous day our spirits were low. Unable to take off during the night meant that we should not now reach Libreville on schedule, though with luck we might still catch our connection with only hours to spare. We flew above the murk, which cleared before we reached the high ground of the Fernando Po. We touched down on the long grass strip of Libreville with the hot, stinking clammy air wafting onto our faces through the open side windows. As we refuelled in readiness for an early take-off two natives clad only in loin cloths strolled near the Gemini. Upon the shoulder of one rested a bamboo pole on the end of which was tied a dead monkey. His companion had a smaller pole and skewered to this was a bloody mess that at first glance looked like a decapitated seagull. As we watched them amble by I turned to Jacko and joked: "There goes our supper, Jacko." There never was a truer word said in jest.

When Jacko asked our scruffy-looking native to drive his decrepit vehicle to the best hotel we had the shock of our lives. Leaving the primitive airstrip the broken-down Renault crawled along narrow sandy tracks that wound through the jungle. On the way we passed numerous shacks and dwellings in which poor white and black mixed happily as family units, or so it appeared. Eventually we came to a larger but equally filthy and decrepit building on the front of which hung a broken sign, the lettering long since fallen victim to the heat and humidity. As we pressed through the motley collection of drunken humanity that blocked the entrance our first reaction was to return to the aircraft. But having stepped off the Gemini pouring with perspiration, and having had nothing to eat since five in the morning, we would have given anything to have a cool drink and a cold shower.

The best thing that could be said about our hotel room is that it was large and contained two double beds. On arrival Jacko had made a beeline for the bathroom and I heard him let out a gasp followed quickly by an oath. As I walked quickly to him he was trying to wash some creepy crawlies down a hole in the concrete floor with a tepid spray the colour of cocoa. The dirty towels were badly worn and stank and so we used our handkerchiefs to wipe our faces. We decided to live with our discomfort until we reached the luxury of our accommodation in Leopoldville. With some apprehension we felt our way down a bare wooden stairway dimly lit by a single fly-stained bulb to a large reception area, where a filthy and slovenly French manageress greeted us. As the door opened we were struck by a foul smell of body odour and stale wine. Inside, the temperature was even higher than the suffocating humidity outside.

The large smoke-filled room was crowded with Portuguese, French, Italians and Negroes sitting around small tables on which slopped beer and other potent drinks. The atmosphere was so filled with smoke that it was impossible to see from one end of the room to the other. We sat on rickety chairs at the first empty table we could find, keeping our elbows well away from the slop in front of us. Jacko gave me a nudge and I turned to see a huge bowl of meat and vegetables, with large bones overlapping the sides, being taken by a Negro dressed in a dirty red vest and torn shorts that may well have been underpants. Jacko and I looked at each other and without another word we made our way back to the bedroom. On the way we came across a door that opened on to what we assumed to be the kitchen, and we could not resist peering inside. The atmosphere was worse than anything I had ever seen. Smoke poured from wood fires and bodies of animals were being brutally butchered by sweating natives wielding machetes upon sheets of steel plate laid across two trestles. The sight was nauseating and we quickly shut the door before vomiting.

Back in our squalid bedroom we searched our holdalls for something that would get rid of the putrescent odour that seemed to persist in our nostrils. We found one overripe banana, which we pulled in half, a small piece of Terry's motoring chocolate well melted into the silver paper, and a small packet of biscuits. We debated whether or not to go out to the Gemini and sleep in the cockpit. On consideration we thought it unwise with all the drunken roughnecks around. Finally we decided to keep our clothes on and lie on the sordid bed, using our holdalls to keep our heads from the filth from so many bodies that had occupied the beds before us. I am not sure that either of us slept at all that night. I do know that we were up and checking the Gemini at first light.

After take-off we were soon climbing above the usual low cloud and mist of the jungle to set course in the clear air for Leopoldville. Our interruptions at Agadir and Takoradi left us with only hours to spare to catch the Pan-American flight to Johannesburg. This meant that we would have to deliver the Gemini to Leopoldville and not directly to van Lancker at Kolo. I was a little sorry about this because I wanted Jacko to meet this remarkable family.

As we touched down at Leopoldville I turned to shake hands with Jacko on a mission completed. He was peering with bloodshot eyes and with several days' growth of beard into an old pocket looking-glass we carried in our emergency case. "My God," he said, "if I arrive home in this state Ruth will give me hell."

Later, refreshed and clean, I left Jacko and returned to the airport and the Gemini where all the van Lancker family had arrived to greet me. They were more than delighted with the aircraft and, after checking the spares and showing them the wooden propeller strapped inside the fuselage, I excused myself to go and confirm my departure in the morning for Johannesburg.

After the initial excitement of my return everyone wanted to hear my news of the collapse of the Miles Aircraft company. The first reaction was of sadness and bitter disappointment. General Mining was however involved with so many activities that any despondency quickly gave way to enthusiasm for the next new exciting venture. I thought of my moral obligations to those trusting people with whom I had negotiated sales, but inwardly I felt that the Woodley factory would run for some time under the Receiver and that the spare parts situation would not become a problem for some considerable time, if at all. Both Ian Hay and I felt sad and concerned for those friends in England who had suffered from this calamity from which, in commercial terms, they might never recover. For myself I regarded that final month in Johannesburg to be a bustling, active and at times tense period during our preparations to leave that hot, tawdry and raw city. I carried out my office work normally and when my future plans were discussed at board meetings they were brushed aside with the comment: "Oh, you'll soon change your mind when you get over there!"

The final exodus was helped by the fact that Barbara and I had, for some months, been making fairly comprehensive plans. These included purchasing and storing furniture and carpets, most of which were sent by boat in time for our arrival in England. We were fortunate to have one of the company's Dakotas at our disposal. These aircraft, as I have already mentioned, were filled to capacity on the southbound flight, but in winter they were empty for the return flight to the UK. I was therefore able to load a substantial quantity of the more expensive carpets, light furniture and clothing on board without inconvenience to anyone.

Our early morning departure from Germiston on February 21st 1948 in Dakota ZS-BCA was quiet and subdued, and without comment. My immediate friends regarded it as just another UK jaunt from which they assumed we would return wiser and content to settle in a wonderful land that had so much to offer. Of all my associates in the Transvaal I think only Ian Hay really understood my innermost feelings. I am quite sure that given different circumstances he would have jumped at the opportunity of returning with us.

The Dakota, in spite of its wartime accommodation, was not uncomfortable and we certainly had plenty of space to stretch our legs. All of us were familiar with the country over which we were now flying and there was little of interest to attract our attention, though little Alex was still excited and alert as he trotted down the cabin to the unpartitioned cockpit. I had a clear view through the starboard window but was lost in thought as I watched the narrow dark green ribbon of the River Limpopo twisting and turning beneath us.

We were saying goodbye to the Union of South Africa and might never see it again. I wondered if I was doing the right thing, not for myself, but for Barbara and Alex. I felt no qualms about our departure from Johannesburg. In spite of all the good things and the advantages it had to offer I was certain that apartheid would ultimately bring tragedy to both blacks and whites alike. With an intelligent and wise administration, I felt there was hope. But I had seen enough of the stiff-necked, puritanical and bigoted Boers to realise that those stubborn and in many ways stupid Overlanders, with their own particular brand of appraisal, would shape a situation that would only lead to disaster. Where and when, though, I knew not.

Months later, I happened to be strolling down Regent Street in London and almost walked straight into Ken Waller, a former pilot with Miles Aircraft at Reading. "My God, Alex," he exclaimed, "how extraordinary to run into you like this. Did you know that the Air Ministry had been trying to contact you? They say they have received a statement from the French Air Ministry accusing you of being responsible for what could have been an incident between our two countries. We were only informed because they thought you were still a director of Miles."

More than 40 years later Barbara and I were having dinner with Ruth and Jacko in their beautiful retreat up in the hills overlooking Wellington in New Zealand. I asked Jacko what he remembered best of our flight in Gemini OO-CDP in 1948. Without hesitation he replied: "Me sweating blood as I saw the hangar lights come on, the men rushing to the gun emplacements and the expectation of machine-gun bullets carving us up at any second, while Alex stood alongside the fuselage and had the longest pee on record."

# January 6th–12th 1948, in Miles Gemini OO-CDP

| Date | From | To | Time | | Remarks |
|------|------|-----|----|----|---------|
| January 6 | Woodley | Lympne | 1 | 00 | |
| January 7 | Lympne | Bordeaux | 4 | 45 | Picked up Lorentz at Lympne |
| " | Bordeaux | San Sebastian | 1 | 45 | |
| " | San Sebastian | Bilbao | | 40 | |
| " | Bilbao | Biarritz | | 45 | |
| January 8 | Biarritz | Madrid | 2 | 30 | |
| " | Madrid | Rabat | 4 | 30 | |
| " | Rabat | Agadir | 2 | 00 | |
| January 9 | Agadir | Cape Juby | 1 | 45 | |
| " | Cape Juby | Villa Cisneros | 2 | 15 | |
| " | Villa Cisneros | Port Étienne | 2 | 15 | |
| " | Port Étienne | Bathurst | 5 | 15 | |
| January 10 | Bathurst | Freetown | 4 | 30 | Freetown fogbound |
| " | Freetown | Robertsport | 3 | 15 | |
| " | Robertsport | Takoradi | 6 | 45 | |
| January 11 | Takoradi | Port Harcourt | 6 | 30 | |
| " | Port Harcourt | Libreville | 4 | 15 | |
| January 12 | Libreville | Leopoldville | 5 | 30 | |
| January 13 | Leopoldville | Kolo | 1 | 15 | |
| | | **Total Flying Time** | 61 | 25 | |

**Left,** on February 21, 1948 Dakota ZS-BCA was loaded up with the Henshaw's carpets, furniture and baggage for the return trip to England. Here the author and his son Alex pause by the entrance to the Dakota prior to leaving Johannesburg for the last time. The family had the aircraft entirely to themselves for the journey home. (Author).

**Below,** A.V. Air Transport's Douglas Dakota ZS-BCA, in which the author returned to the UK in February 1948 on completion of his appointment with Miles Aircraft of South Africa (Pty.) Ltd. (Roger T. Jackson).

*After acquiring his pilot's licence the author's son purchased this Beech 35 Bonanza.*

*The author and his son Alex with the latter's Beech 35 Bonanza.*

# AFTER AFRICA

I must confess that ten years of hard relentless effort in a country struggling to come to terms with the aftermath of war, in an atmosphere already becoming stifled by the straight-jacket of Socialist bureaucracy, was demoralising. As I have already described in the epilogue to the recent updating of my book *Sigh for a Merlin*, those early postwar days were the most difficult and demanding of my whole life.

By 1953 the whole of our family organisation, with the exception of the farms which were still held by tenanted occupants, was beginning to respond and the horizon looked distinctly brighter. The North Sea flood of January 31st 1953, however, was as near mortal as a blow can get. Thousands of homes were devastated or destroyed and hundreds of men, women and children drowned. Farmland was put out of viable production for at least five years. With land, interests and property in five coastal parishes, including the Sutton-on-Sea 18-hole golf course, it was obvious that my family should be hurt worse than most. It was at the peak of the disaster for those in its forefront that one was able to observe humanity 'stripped to the bone.' Whilst the disaster certainly brought out the best in people it also brought out the worst. For my part I was just grateful that my wife and family had survived.

By 1957 my father was of retiring age and there is no doubt that the departure to war of three sons, resulting in the death of his youngest boy, did much to hasten the decline of his health. This was to impose an unexpected additional load upon my shoulders. My wife Barbara was to prove a wonderful and remarkable partner during the struggle to revitalise so much that had suffered the ravages of war. Without her eagerness to share responsibility and offer intelligent and practical ideas and suggestions, coupled with the determination to rise above all the vicissitudes of our day-to-day life, I am certain the success ultimately achieved would not have taken place.

So many people have asked me why I gave up serious flying so soon, and did I not miss the excitement and challenge of fresh fields in a modernised world? A quick answer would have to be, yes, I did. Perhaps the most important factor was that I was no longer compelled to subject my wife to the mental anguish and stress that she had borne silently and for so long. During more than six years of war she had been in close proximity of screaming Spitfires and roaring Lancasters, with grim knowledge and experience of her own horrific moments of death in the air. Now our aim was to erase the scars of war and I more or less promised that I would not be tempted by further challenges in the air and would give up flying all together. I realised at the time that I would not find this easy. I had many good friends in Supermarine and the offer to fly for them whenever I had the time was a most tempting and generous proposal. However, apart from the consideration for my wife, common sense prevailed. To fly to the highest standards one has to be fully prepared mentally and physically. As it was, the demands within my own commercial organisation were complex and difficult, involving in some instances releases of large blocks of properties impounded by the Army and the Navy on outbreak of war. The negotiations for their release were difficult and tedious, with time-consuming discussions and meetings with local and county councils. Endless new rules and regulations seemed to have arisen since my departure in September 1939. I was more than aware that I could not immerse myself in two distinctly different jobs at the same time and expect to achieve satisfactory results. As it turned out, although our home was wrecked amidst total devastation, ten years later few would have realised that there had ever been such a catastrophe.

Above all else my family always came first. From the earliest age our son Alex was at our side and in so far as was possible was always treated as an adult. The happiest days were those when he could participate in mature, more masculine, sports in which he could give a good account of himself. Some of the finest moments would be sailing our 505 dinghy from the open beach after the sea had been 'roughed' up by a storm and leaving as much wind as we could handle. It was sailing as demanding and exciting as it was possible to get in the North Sea. Alex was never competitive with his skiing but I envied his ability and style from an early age in that deep powder snow that comes up to the armpits provided by the Canadian Rockies. As he grew older Alex inevitably drove fast cars, which he did with skill and a quite unexpected maturity. I do not think I have ever been driven so fast and yet so safely.

After travelling the world for a year following the pressures of education and training, Alex, now a qualified chartered accountant, decided to take the senior managerial position of Financial Director with the family organisation. It was one of those moments that I suppose all parents pray for.

Though still heavily involved with business Barbara and I were now able to create more interests abroad, content that the overall control of our companies was in competent hands during our absence. It was during this period that Alex asked if I would object if he took up flying. I am sure that he already assumed that I would be secretly pleased, but he was not so sure about his mother. When I broached the subject to Barbara she, to my delight, said: "He has his own life to live, I am not going to stand in his way." Thus it was that I drifted back, albeit in a minor way, into a field of interest and activity that I had missed so much since I flew my last Spitfire in January 1946.

As expected, Alex carried out and completed his training at Kidlington,

Oxford without any problems. The first aircraft he bought was a Piper Arrow, and then after a year or so he went to the USA and purchased a new Beech Bonanza. Long range tanks were fitted to the Bonanza and it was flown across the Atlantic back to Britain via Greenland.

I discovered that flying in the Bonanza with my son, mostly over Europe and North Africa, was a far cry from the times I had flown with my father, when we would often fly off the beaten track in the Percival Vega Gull and put down on the Hungarian steppes, or some other remote and primitive spot in jungle or desert. Those days had long since gone. The regulatory control, prohibited areas and general restrictions had taken out all the adventurous interludes enjoyed by amateurs like myself. The warmth of reception and congeniality had also disappeared and one had the impression that light private aircraft were tolerated, but not willingly. In my experience the more minor the official the more autocratic his demeanour, so that every landing at a strange airport was carried out with a degree of apprehension and speculation. The basic training, certainly in my son's case, was excellent and he was soon flying to airline standard, whereas in my flying days it took years to acquire the experience necessary to competently handle an aircraft in limited flying conditions.

One day, soon after Alex had completed his training, we were flying from Malta to Dubrovnik in perfect cloudless conditions when Brindisi warned of severe weather ahead. Although some aircraft were taking off from Dubrovnik, most were grounded. I facetiously but foolishly quipped to Alex that we would now see how good his training had been. We entered heavy, turbulent black cumulous cloud about a hundred miles from Dubrovnik. The airport control would not permit a direct approach for 15 to 20 minutes and we were stacked in very unpleasant storm conditions. I certainly felt uncomfortable over such mountainous country and I was unable to listen to the instructions from Dubrovnik control. When eventually we were given landing instructions we were in thick cloud and heavy rain. We had started our descent from 8,000 ft on instruments and I kept an alert silence as Alex concentrated and listened to instructions that were given in broken English and not easy to understand. By the time the altimeter registered 500 ft I must confess I was becoming apprehensive. Then, hardly discernible in the murk, the dulled lights of the runway showed ahead and just beneath our wheels, and Alex made a perfect landing.

* * * * * * * * *

It is now over 73 years since I first went solo in a DH Gipsy Moth 1. Most of my friends have read and heard the phrase "The Golden Years of Flying" and I am continually asked what was so marvellous about them. This query cannot be answered in a few words, but essentially it was the freedom to roam the skies in aircraft about which we knew so little and which, if misused, could be very dangerous indeed.

It was a tremendous 'fun' period in that all of us were amateurs, whether we were in the RAF, commercial flying, the owner of an aircraft or just an enthusiastic onlooker cadging rides whenever the opportunity arose. The result of this was that every so often this cosmopolitan crowd would meet and mix on equal terms to discuss the latest achievement in aviation or – as so often happened – the death or injury of some hapless pilot or friend. Flying in those days was not unlike riding a bicycle: once you had mastered the basics you would never forget.

Good friends provided me with a Puss Moth flight to mark my 80th birthday: but the short, though enjoyable, exercise was so simple and easy that it was not worthy of special note. Again, ten years later, loyal friends provided me with three different types of aircraft to mark my 90th birthday. I did not like flying the Tiger Moth because I sat too low in the cockpit to find a visual focal point on which to orientate, and it was also very draughty. Best of all I enjoyed the Pitts Special, but for aerobatics I prefer the Spitfire or Arrow Active, although I do accept that the light and rapid control response of the Pitts made it more spectacular and easier to control, although I found inverted flying no problem, which indeed did surprise me. The main thing that affected me, and something that needed care and caution, was any manoeuvre that created 'g' loads; in my younger flying days I would normally pull 7 'g' before 'blacking out' but now I was acutely aware when in only 4 or 5 'g'.

I am by nature a strong disciplinarian and appreciate law and order, but having been brought up by my father to manage and control a wide range of commercial undertakings, I understand that there is a wide difference between using discipline for efficient control to achieve success and 'flooding' an organisation with petty controls and restrictions that not only overload the organisation with non-productive procedures but in the end destroy it as profits turn into liabilities.

This applies equally well in aviation today. It is vital to have very strict controls and discipline in all facets of aviation, and much of what has been incorporated has been successful. Today however there is the grave danger of training pilots only to operate within a system where every move is directed by Control. The pilot that complies with every rule is competent until something goes wrong which is beyond the realms of his training, and then in so many cases the pilot does not respond as he should – he has been directed for so long that he has lost the ability to initiate a move on his own. This is reflected in a number of incidents and fatalities at air displays recently: a simple forced landing due to engine failure is often catastrophic, and this in turn leads to the introduction of even more rules and regulations.

From my experience the early days of flying after the Great War amounted to an exploration of the sky by those who knew so little. As a result it taught pilots responsibility and an awareness of what might – and could – happen if something unforeseen or unexpected arose.

The key to safe and satisfactory flying is – and indeed always has been – self-discipline and common sense.

* * * * * * * * * *

Most people of my generation were brought up within a strong family unit. We had a responsible father and mother to give us advice and guidance and a set of standards not to be broken. When my first book, *Sigh for a Merlin,* was published in the 1970s I wrote: "There are some gifts in life that are beyond price – although we are not always aware of them at the time. My wife Barbara was married under the rapid thud of gunfire, the rat-tat-tat of machine guns and the scream of diving aircraft. She has now walked beside me for 40 years – and she, more than anyone, knows the sorrow, the pain and the frustration that has been part of our life, but she has also been there to receive the applause, the success and the rewards that have come our way. Our son, Alex, is the culmination of this wonderful partnership."

My wife died eight years ago after a partnership of 58 years. I know that she would have wished me to conclude by adding the following:

"The greatest joy of all is to know that our only son has been blessed with those qualities held so dearly but rarely encountered today: integrity, loyalty, patriotism and a filial duty carried out with warmth, compassion and a depth of love to his parents that has made our old age worthwhile."

# APPENDIX

The following pages, compiled by Richard Riding, outline briefly the design, development and handling characteristics of the three main aircraft types flown by the author during his period in South Africa, namely, the Miles M.38 Messenger, Miles M.65 Gemini and de Havilland DH.104 Dove. Each description includes a three-view general arrangement drawing in addition to data tables giving details of dimensions and performance. The histories and ultimate fates of specific aircraft flown by the author are included at the end of each section.

## THE MILES M.38 MESSENGER

The Miles M.38 Messenger's origins date back to 1939, the year that George Miles began designing a replacement for the successful three-seat Miles M.17 Monarch and the earlier two-seat Miles M.11 Whitney Straight. The war put paid to further progress but in 1941 the demand for a service training and communications aircraft prompted George Miles to pick up where he had left off. He came up with the design for a safe and easy-to-fly trainer that embodied all the latest requirements of modern military aircraft, such as retractable undercarriage, constant speed propeller and flaps. Under the supervision of George Miles, project engineer Ray Bournon carried out the detail design. The resulting aircraft was a low-wing, four-seat monoplane with split trailing edge flaps and a retractable undercarriage.

The first flight of the prototype Miles M.28, U-0232, was made by George Miles on July 11th 1941. It was the first light aeroplane type to be designed and built by any British company during the war years. Capable of carrying four people at 160 m.p.h. for 500 miles on only 140 hp, the M.28 had a great deal of promise. It was the company's intention to put the M.28 into quantity production after the war but this plan was abandoned in favour of the Messenger, Gemini and Aerovan and only six M.28s were built.

The story could have ended there had it not been for the fact that the M.28's short-field performance and unequalled field of view had impressed a group of Army officers. In September 1942 Miles was asked to design a similar machine for Air Observation Post duties, providing it could be produced at very short notice. The Army's list of requirements included the following stipulations: the aircraft had to be easy to fly and be capable of taking off from small or unprepared fields, bounded by trees. In addition to carrying a crew of two, plus parachutes, it had to carry a radio transmitter and receiver – large items in those days – and armour plate. In the air it was essential for the pilot and observer to have uninterrupted views in all directions and maintenance had to be carried out by unskilled personnel. This was a tall order by any standards.

Produced as a private venture the problem was tackled in typical mercurial Miles fashion. Using the fuselage of the prototype M.28 George Miles fitted a one-piece wing of 6ft greater span and added non-retractable flaps. The twin-fin layout and the one-piece moulded Perspex windscreen were retained but longer stroke undercarriage legs were fitted. Just three months later George Miles successfully flew U-0223, the prototype M.38. The only major modification required was the addition of a central fin to improve low-speed directional control. With a take-off run of less than 75 yd and a stalling speed of about 30 mph the Miles M.38 Messenger appeared to be the answer to the Army's prayer.

Unfortunately, because the Army had gone to Miles via the back door and not through official but time-consuming channels, a battle was sparked off between the War Office and the Ministry of Production. This resulted in the Army being denied an immediate order for 100 Messengers and the service was thus deprived of an eminently suitable aircraft. Eventually the Ministry of Aircraft Production placed an order for the Messenger to Specification 17/43 for use as a liaison and VIP aircraft with the RAF, but only 21 Messengers from the original order for 250 were produced.

Proof of the suitability and reliability of the Messenger Mk 1, *and* its 140 hp de Havilland Gipsy Major engine, can be judged by the fact that examples were put at the disposal of such personages as Winston Churchill, Field Marshal Bernard Montgomery – who used the Messenger to tour forward battle areas – and Marshal of the RAF Lord Tedder.

Made entirely of wood, the Messenger had a fabric-covered resin-bonded stressed ply skin throughout. The fuselage, comprising two main sections, the cabin and a rear semi-monocoque, was built up on four longerons and stringers with U-frames. The one-piece wing consisted of twin box spars and ribs, with provision for the single 18-gallon capacity fuel tank in the starboard root: a second tank in the port root was optional. The fixed cantilever single-strut undercarriage legs, each with rear shock absorber leg, were designed to withstand intentional heavy short-field landings, and the tailwheel was of the fixed castoring type. Early Messengers were fitted with fixed-pitch wooden propellers. The independently balanced centrally-hinged gull-wing doors afforded easy access to the roomy cockpit.

Though the bulk of the RAF order for Messengers was cancelled at the end of the war, the type enjoyed a new lease of life on the civil market when a definitive civil version (Mk 2A) was put into production in Northern Ireland. Production initially began at a former linen mill at Banbridge, County Down but was later transferred to Newtownards Aerodrome. When completed the unpainted aircraft were flown across to Woodley, Reading for painting and final fitting according to customers' preferences before being sold. In 1946-7 the selling price of a Messenger was £2,500.

**Above,** *the Miles M.28, forerunner of the Miles M.38 Messenger. Note the retractable undercarriage and twin tail unit.* (The Aeroplane photograph).

**Below,** *G-AGPX was a three-seat Miles M.38 Messenger Mk 2B powered by a Blackburn Cirrus Major 3 engine. Note the square rear windows.*

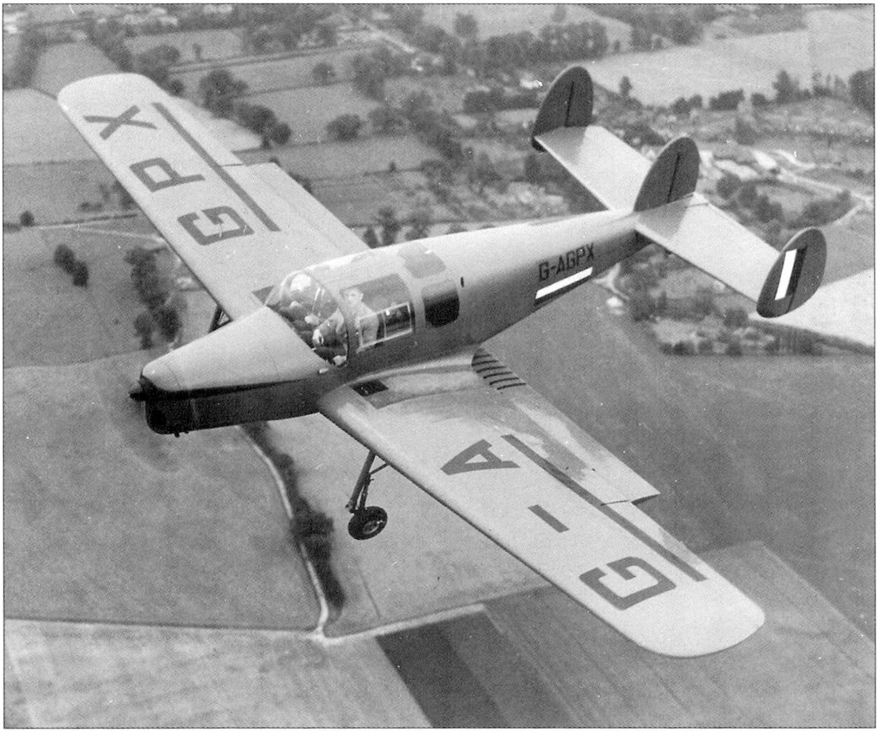

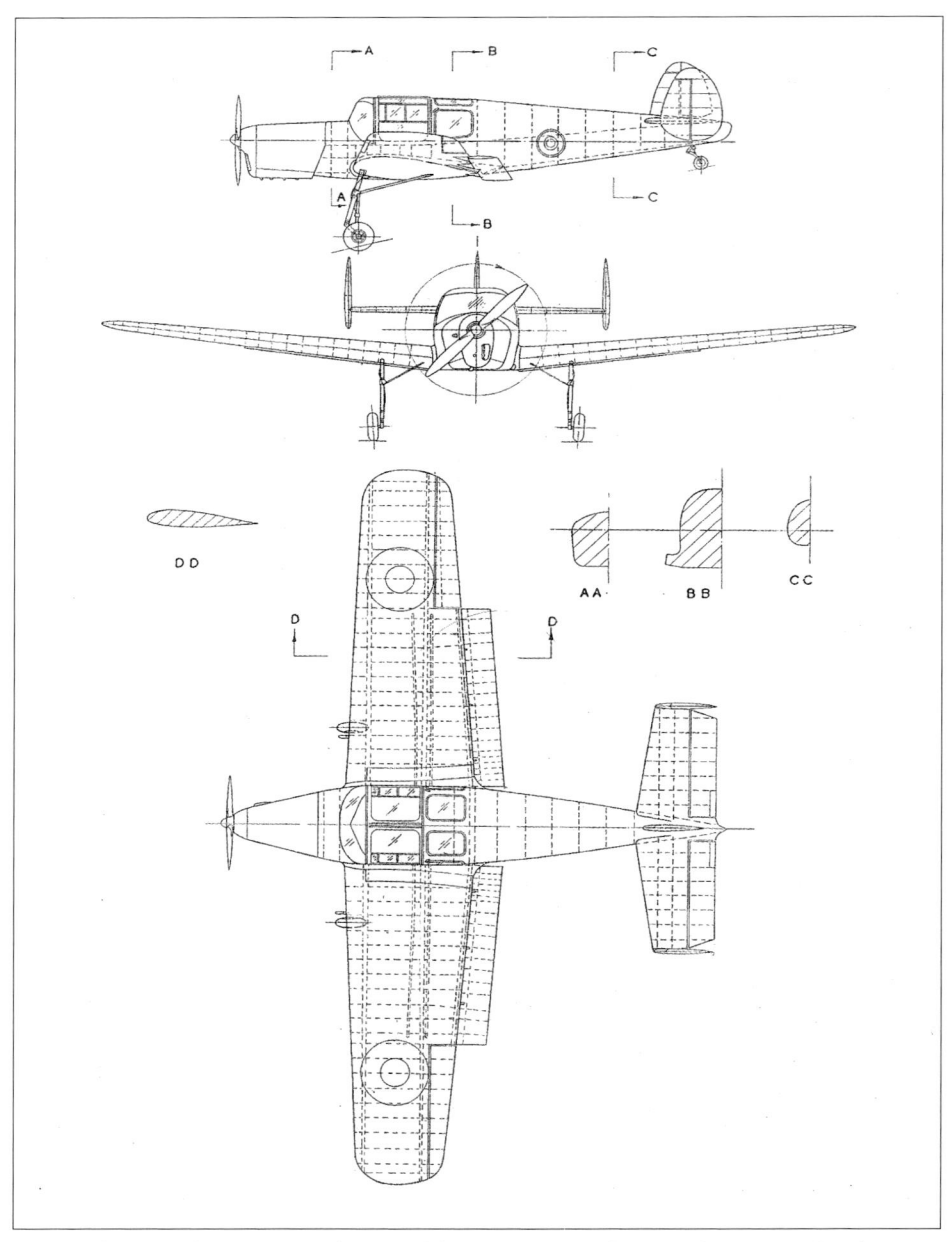

This general arrangement drawing of the DH.104 Dove I by E.J. Riding is reproduced with the permission of *Aeromodeller*.

The only external difference from earlier Messengers was the rear passengers' oval windows – those of the RAF versions being square. The fitting of a 155 hp Blackburn Cirrus Major III engine and a coarser-pitch propeller gave the Messenger an improved cruising speed.

Although production in Ireland finally ceased in January 1948, this was not the end of the Messenger's civil career. That same year the RAF declared all its Messengers surplus to requirements and twenty or so were converted and sold to civil operators during the next couple of years.

Had it not been for the post-war demise of Miles Aircraft the Messenger might well have been produced by the hundreds. Of the 90 or so Miles Messengers built three-quarters were sold in the UK. The first to be sold abroad was the Messenger 2C G-AGUW, powered by a 145 hp de Havilland Gipsy Major 1D engine. Built for demonstration and export in South Africa this was the aircraft flown out from Reading to Johannesburg by the author in March 1946 – see Chapter 3.

Today, in 2004, only a handful of airworthy Messengers survive.

## MILES M.38 MESSENGER DATA

| | |
|---|---|
| **Span:** | 36ft 2in |
| **Length:** | 24ft |
| **Height:** | 7ft 6in |
| **Wing area:** | 191 sq ft |
| **Aspect ratio:** | 6.8 |
| **Weight empty:** | 1,450 lb (Mk. 2A, 2B and 3) 155 hp Blackburn Cirrus Major III, 1,360 lb (Mk. 2C, 4 and 4A) 145 hp de Havilland Gipsy Major 1D/10 |
| **All-up weight:** | 2,400 lb (all marks) |
| **Maximum speed:** | 135 mph (Mk 2A, 2B and 3) 115 mph (Mk 2C, 4 and 4A) |
| **Cruising speed:** | 124 mph (Mk 2A, 2B and 3) 100 mph (Mk 2C, 4 and 4A) |
| **Ceiling:** | 16,000 ft (Mk 2A, 2B and 3) 17,000ft (Mk 2C, 4 and 4A) |
| **Range:** | 460 miles (all marks) |

# DEMONSTRATED BY THE AUTHOR

## Miles Messenger 2C G-AGUW (c/n 6267)

Certificate of Airworthiness issued on February 28th 1946.

The author left Reading (Woodley) with W.P. Salter (ex-ATA and/or Miles) as engineer on March 8th 1946, arriving at Germiston on March 23rd.

Author's last flight in G-AGUW was a test flight after top overhaul prior to delivery to Albert Fischer in the Belgian Congo made on August 3rd 1946.

Later that month G-AGUW was sold to Albert Fischer and delivered to Moanda in the Belgian Congo as OO-CCM. The Messenger crashed on October 10th 1948.

## Miles Messenger 4 G-AHGE (c/n 6330)

Certificate of Airworthiness issued on May 13th 1946.

While engaged upon a sales tour of Europe G-AHGE was diverted to Almaza, Cairo, arriving there on September 22nd, where it was met by the author. The following day the author took off from Almaza with three Greek passengers, and after dropping them off at Ndola on September 26th he arrived at Germiston the following day – see Chapter 6.

Author's last flight in G-AHGE was when he delivered it from Germiston to new owner Charles Taylor at Tugela on October 25th 1946. On the same day the owner's son, John, wrote off the aircraft after hitting a cable strung across a river whilst low flying!

## MILES M.65 GEMINI

With the Miles M.38 Messenger in production in Northern Ireland the Miles brothers and their staff found themselves undertaking long over-water trips between Woodley and Ireland in single-engined aircraft. George Miles set about designing a one-off twin-engined four-seater purely for their use. In order to save time and to keep costs to a minimum the Messenger was re-designed to take two four-cylinder in-line air-cooled 100 hp Blackburn Cirrus engines and to accommodate a retractable undercarriage. Many Messenger components were retained, though the empennage reverted to the twin-fin configuration of the earlier M.28.

Fred Miles made the first flight of the prototype Miles M.65 Gemini, G-AGUS, with fixed undercarriage, from Woodley on October 26th 1945. The flying characteristics of the Gemini were, not unnaturally, very similar to those of the popular Messenger. It had light and harmonious controls, making it easy and safe to fly. In addition to having a reasonably fast cruising speed the Gemini had relatively slow stalling and landing speeds, qualities that made it eminently suitable for the private owner. The decision was taken to put the "one-off" into production.

Like that of the Messenger the fuselage of the Gemini was of plastic-bonded plywood construction. Because of its higher wing loading and landing speed there was no necessity to retain the central fin and rudder. The engines were mounted beneath the cantilever one-piece wing to facilitate servicing, thus providing an unbroken wing surface. The spacious 4 ft-wide cabin, with characteristic Miles high-visibility moulded one-piece Perspex windscreen and centrally-hinged gull-winged doors, offered space and luxury hitherto out of financial reach for the private owner. A luggage compartment behind the hinged nose could accommodate up to four suitcases. Initially doped in overall cream with red or green trim and registration letters, the Gemini was an attractive buy, though the high gloss finish soon took on the characteristic wrinkled appearance that befell many plywood covered aircraft of the period.

Known for its light and harmonious controls and its innocuous stall the Gemini had no vices, though the unwary found it had a tendency to swing on take-off, easily corrected with use of full rudder and juggling with the throttles. During early testing it was found almost impossible to execute a three-point landing in the prototype Gemini. It was soon discovered that the wing centre-section stalled first and caused a turbulent airflow which reduced the effectiveness of the elevators; the addition of wing leading edge slats inboard of the engine nacelles cured the problem.

Excluding the prototype ten different marks of Gemini were produced, fitted with a variety of Blackburn Cirrus or de Havilland Gipsy Major engines ranging in power from 100 to 155 h.p. The basic airframe remained unchanged, though the Miles M.75 Aries produced independently by Fred Miles in 1950 was powered by two Blackburn Cirrus Major III engines, had a strengthened structure and fins and rudders of larger area. The performance of the Aries was superior to its earlier relatives, often criticised for their marginal performance on one engine with any load.

Expensively priced at a snip under £4,000 the Gemini nevertheless attracted favourable attention and orders were quickly forthcoming, so much so that they rapidly outpaced those for the Messenger. Early production aircraft were designated Gemini 1A and began coming off the production line during the summer of 1946, and within a year around 130 had been built. Because of production problems at Woodley, where the Gemini shared the same production line as the Miles M.57 Aerovan, Miles was unable to keep up with the orders. Though it had been estimated that there was a market for 500 Geminis the company went bankrupt and aircraft production ceased in 1948. Around 140 airframes had been assembled by this time, though a further ten were built subsequently. Sadly the Gemini was Miles' final aircraft to achieve large-scale production.

After the Miles Aircraft company folded, sets of Gemini components survived and were subsequently assembled by other organisations, including two by Handley Page (Reading) Ltd, who had taken over production of the Miles M.60 Marathon airliner. This took the final number of Geminis produced to 150. Though a fifth of these were built for export, two thirds of those registered initially in Britain eventually found their way overseas. One of those exported immediately was G-AILK, flown to Australia by Grp Capt A.F. 'Bush' Bandidt, its arrival in January 1947 marking the first postwar solo flight from Great Britain. A few months later, in April, the author flew Gemini G-AISD from Woodley to Johannesburg – see Chapter 7.

With hindsight it is doubtful that the wooden Gemini could have staved off the looming competition from America, but for several years it was in a world class of its own. The introduction of the Piper Apache in the early 1950s heralded mass-production of cheaper *metal* twins from the modern plants of Messrs Beech, Cessna and Piper. The technology was there at Woodley, with the building of the prototype Marathon airliners, but by 1948 the question was academic. At the time of the Miles collapse work was progressing on a five-seat all-metal development of the Gemini, but with heavy production costs the new tricycle undercarriage Gemini replacement would perhaps have been out of reach of all but the very wealthy.

Of the total of 150 or so Geminis produced less than a handful remain airworthy in 2004. One of them, soon to become G-AISD again, is the very machine that the author ferried from Lympne to Germiston back in January 1947!

# MILES M.65 GEMINI 1A DATA

| | |
|---|---|
| **Wing span:** | 36 ft 2 in |
| **Length:** | 22 ft 3in |
| **Height:** | 7 ft 6in |
| **Wing area:** | 191 sq ft |
| **Aspect ratio:** | 6.8 |
| **Weight empty:** | 1,773 lb |
| **All-up weight:** | 3,000 lb |
| **Wing loading:** | 15.7 lb/sq ft |
| **Distance to unstick:** | 110 yds in 5 mph wind |
| **Distance to 50ft:** | 215 yds in 5 mph wind |
| **Initial climb rate:** | 550 ft per min |
| **Maximum speed:** | 146 mph |
| **Cruising speed:** | 131 mph |
| **Stalling speed:** | 35 mph (flaps and undercarriage down) |
| **Rate of climb:** | 606 ft per min |
| **Ceiling:** | 11,300 ft |
| **Range:** | 820 miles |
| **Endurance:** | 8 hr 24 min (at max endurance power) |

## BRIEF HISTORIES OF MILES GEMINIS FERRIED AND DEMONSTRATED BY THE AUTHOR

### Miles Gemini 1A G-AISD (c/n 6285).

Built at Woodley in October 1946 and C. of A. issued on April 3rd 1947.

The author departed Reading for Germiston, Johannesburg on April 3rd 1947. Forced landing at Maldon, Essex on the same day while flying from RAF Strubby to Lympne. Arrived Germiston on April 13th.

The author's last flight in G-AISD was on May 20th 1947 on a demonstration flight at Germiston.

Gemini sold to Southern Aircraft (East Africa) Limited of Fort Ternan, Kenya and registered VP-KDH in June 1947. In 1952 the Gemini suffered a wheels-up landing and it was returned to the UK for repair and overhaul by Miles and reverted briefly to G-AISD. Delivered to Colonel R. Lallemant DFC in Belgium and re-registered OO-RLD, and remained in his ownership until purchased by John Homewood in 1984. It returned to the UK and underwent restoration at Exeter, being restored as G-AISD. It was then returned to Guy Valvekens in Belgium, until 2003 when it was purchased by William Tomkins in the UK.

## Miles Gemini ZS-BRV (c/n 6301).

Built at Woodley and ferried to Germiston, South Africa by Group Captain Macdougall in mid-1947. Test-flown at Germiston by the author on June 6th 1947, and flown extensively by him on sales tours – see Chapter 8. Stored at Port Elizabeth Museum, South Africa from 1969. Passed to South African Air Force Museum, Pretoria in 1979 and believed to be still extant.

## Miles Gemini OO-CDP (c/n 6480).

Built at Woodley in 1947. Delivered to Leopoldville from Woodley by the author, accompanied by Jack Lorentz, January 6th-12th 1948 – see Chapter 10 (subject of cover illustration).

The author's last flight in OO-CDP took place on January 13th 1948 when he handed the Gemini over to new owner van Lancker at Kolo.

**Above,** *unlike production aircraft the prototype Miles M.65 Gemini G-AGUS had a fixed undercarriage.* (The Aeroplane photograph).

**Below,** *the second prototype Miles M.65 Gemini Mk 1A, G-AIDO, flying with its port Blackburn Cirrus engine stopped in December 1946.*

**Left,** *a crane somewhere in South Africa hoists aloft Gemini ZS-BRV, minus its rear fuselage and empennage. The Gemini's one-piece wing and engine nacelles are shown to good advantage. This Gemini was passed to the South African Air Force Museum in Pretoria, South Africa in 1979 and was still extant in 2002.*

**Below,** *G-AISD, the Miles Gemini flown from Reading to Germiston by the author in April 1947 was sold to Southern Aircraft (East Africa) Ltd of Fort Ternan, Kenya and re-registered VP-KDH in June 1947.* (Via Roger T. Jackson).

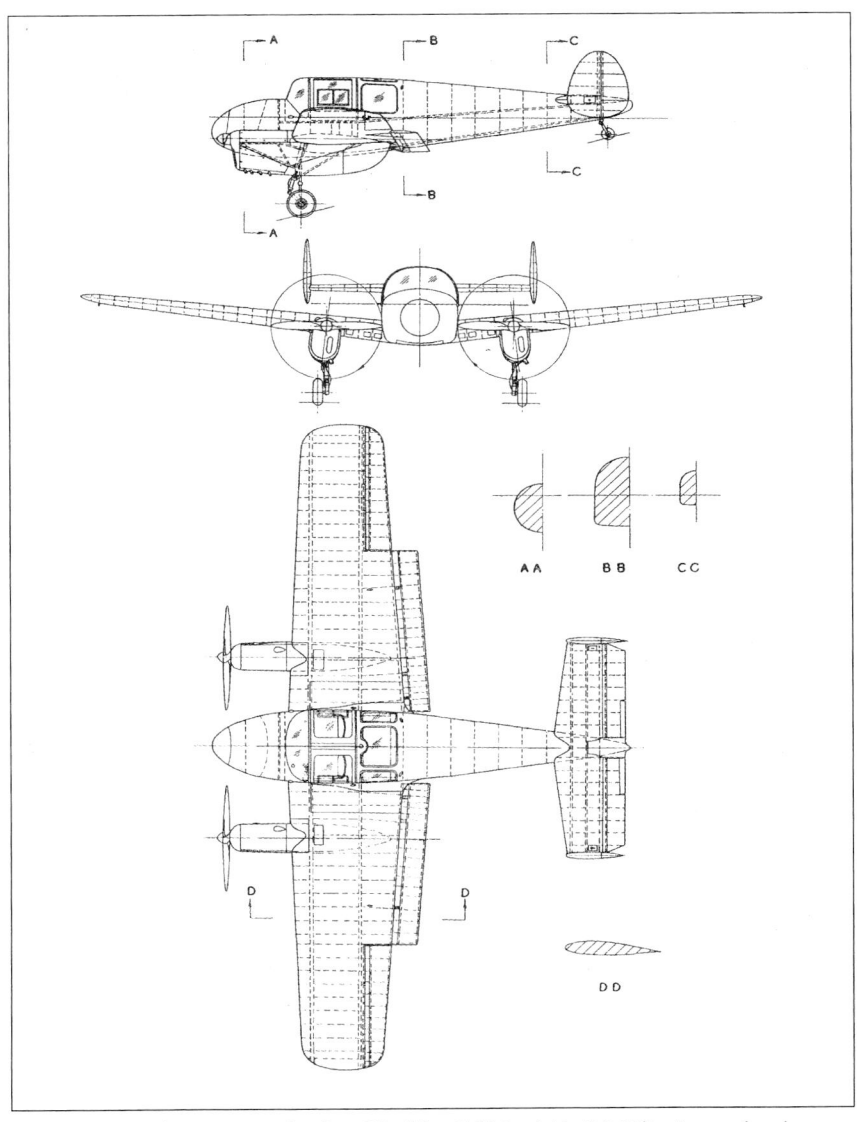

This general arrangement drawing of the Miles M.65 Gemini by E.J. Riding is reproduced with the permission of *Aeromodeller*.

# DE HAVILLAND DH.104 DOVE

Designed by R.E. Bishop, the creator of the Mosquito, and his team as a replacement for the successful de Havilland DH.89 Dragon Rapide, work on the all-metal DH.104 was already in progress at Hatfield during the last months of the Second World War. Designed to the Brabazon Committee's specification 5B for a twin-engined feeder airliner the prototype, G-AGPJ, made its maiden flight on September 25th 1945 in the hands of Geoffrey Pike at Hatfield. De Havilland's first postwar airliner was aptly named Dove and following trials at Farnborough G-AGPJ received several modifications, the most noticeable being the temporary addition of an ugly large slab dorsal fin – soon re-shaped into a graceful curve – to permit a lower single-engine safety speed.

The Dove was an all-metal, twin-engined, low-wing cantilever monoplane with a fully retractable tricycle undercarriage. The single-spar wing was built in two sections and had stressed skin covering. The semi-monocoque fuselage was of oval section and had an entrance door aft on the port side. Luggage was carried beneath the cockpit floor and aft of the cabin with a loading door on the starboard side. The two main wheels retracted outwards, the nose wheel retracted aft. Early Doves were powered by two 330 hp de Havilland Gipsy Queen Series 70 six-cylinder inverted air-cooled engines driving metal three-bladed de Havilland constant speed feathering and braking propellers, making the Dove an entirely de Havilland product. Accommodation was generally for eight passengers and two pilots, all in single seats; two additional seats could be added, three if the toilet was removed.

Initially the Dove's price tag was £14,000, more than three times that of the Gemini. First customers were airlines and within eight months of the first flight export orders for the Dove had reached £2 million. With high efficiency coupled with low operating costs it was evident that the Dove was going to be a runaway success. The Dove also had great passenger appeal, there being plenty of room and effective air-conditioning. The eight large cabin windows, separated by narrow pillars, gave plenty of light in addition to an excellent view. The low-wing lay-out enabled easy loading and with the tops of the engines only 5 ft 9 in from the ground servicing could be carried out without the need for trestles or ladders.

Construction of the Dove was undertaken initially at Hatfield but such was the demand production was moved to Hawarden aerodrome near Chester in 1951. More than 540 Doves were produced, the last variant being the Dove 8 fitted with two 400 hp de Havilland Gipsy Queen 70-3 engines. The Dove 4, a military communications version produced for the RAF from 1948, was known as the Devon C. Mk 1. Dove 4s were supplied to many overseas air forces.

Throughout nearly 20 years of production few changes were made to the Dove. The different mark numbers mostly reflected changes and progressive uprating of the Gipsy Queen 70 engine. The Dove Mks 7 and 8 took on a slightly different appearance when the characteristic Dove transparent fireman's helmet-type cockpit glazing housing the loop and fixed aerials was replaced with a Heron-type canopy, giving an additional five inches of headroom for the pilots.

The Dove gave sterling service overseas and at home for several decades and a handful are still registered in the UK in 2004.

## DE HAVILLAND DH.104 DOVE 1 & 2 DATA

| | |
|---|---|
| **Span:** | 57 ft |
| **Length:** | 39 ft 4 in |
| **Height:** | 13 ft |
| **Wing area:** | 335 sq ft |
| **Aspect ratio:** | 9.7 |
| **Weight empty:** | 5,650 lb |
| **All-up weight:** | 8,500 lb |
| **Initial climb rate:** | 850 ft per min |
| **Maximum speed:** | 201 mph (in level flight) |
| **Cruising speed:** | 165 mph (max cruise) |
| **Rate of climb:** | 750 ft/min (sea level) |
| **Ceiling:** | 20,000 ft |
| **Range:** | 1,000 miles |

# FLOWN BY THE AUTHOR IN 1947

## De Havilland DH.104 Dove 1 ZS-AVH (c/n 04024)

The first two prototype Doves were given the construction numbers 04000/P.1 and 04000/P.2).

ZS-AVH was c/n 04024 and was thus No. 26 off the line. Including the two prototypes 544 Doves of all marks were built at Hatfield and Chester between 1945-1966.

Dove 1 ZS-AVH was owned by AV Air Transport and bore the legend *"Pass the Ammunition Fund"* in English and Afrikaans on the fuselage sides and engine nacelles.

The author began flying ZS-AVH on August 1st 1947 from Germiston.
During a company flight that began at Germiston on August 4th 1947 and took in Elisabethville, Lagos and Libreville, the aircraft was nearly lost when landing at Port Franqui on August 13 – see Chapter 10.

The author's last flight in ZS-AVH was on November 13th 1947 from Germiston.

Dove ZS-AVH was later returned to the UK and become G-AMRN in March 1952. It was later uprated to become the sole Dove Mk 6B and was fitted with two 380 hp de Havilland Gipsy Queen 70-2 engines.

In 1964 G-AMRN was sold in Iceland and re-registered TF-EVM.

**Above**, *G-AGPJ, the first prototype de Havilland DH.104 Dove, made its maiden flight on September 25, 1945 from Hatfield, in the hands of Geoffrey Pike.* (The Aeroplane photograph).

**Above,** *the DH.104 Dove was initially produced at Hatfield but production was moved to Hawarden, Chester in 1951. This 1946 photograph of Doves in production at Hatfield shows an aircraft destined for Central African Airways in the foreground.*

**Above,** *in March 1952 DH.104 Dove ZS-AVH returned to the UK and was registered G-AMRN. This photograph was taken shortly before the aircraft was sold in Iceland in 1964.* (Richard Riding photograph).

**Below,** *the pilot's cockpit and instrument panel of an early production DH.104 Dove.*

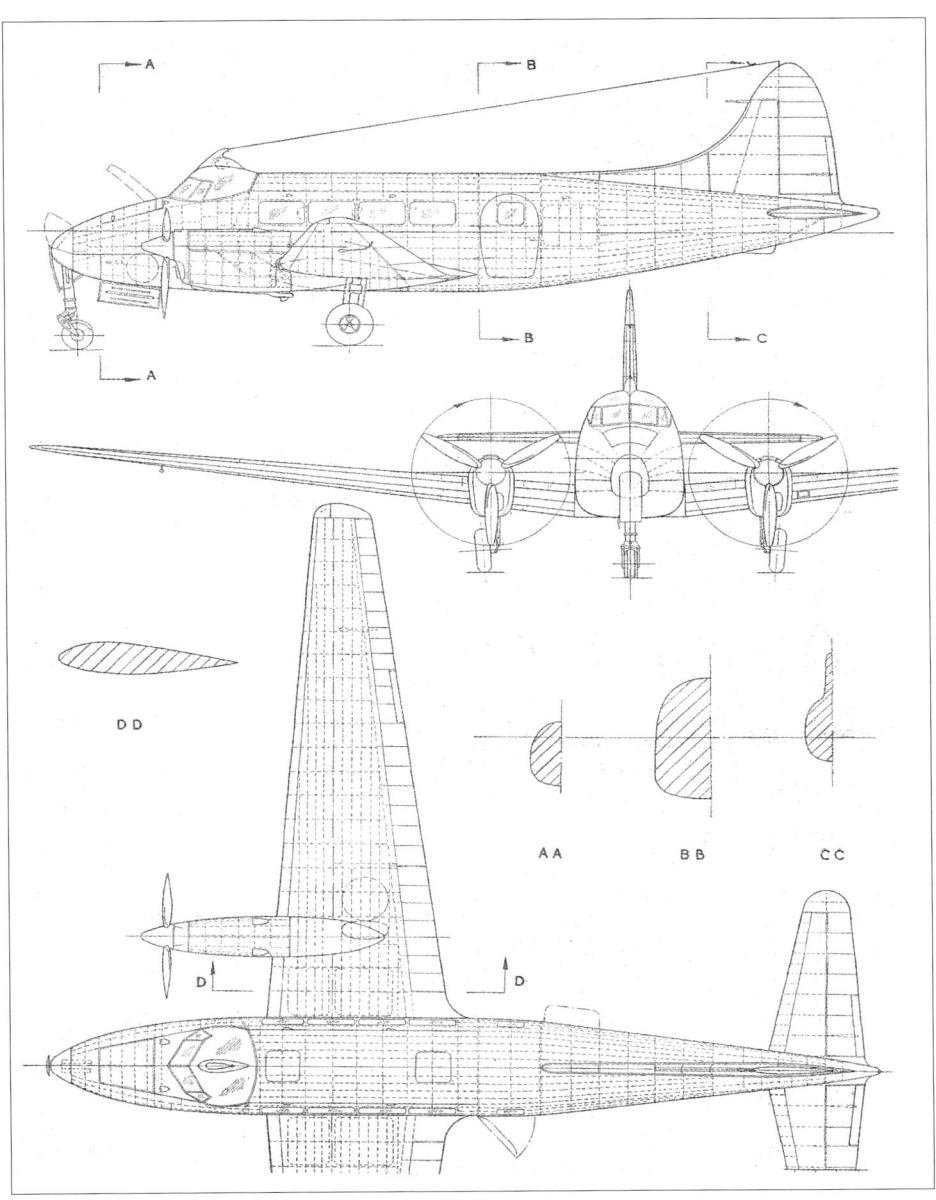

This general arrangement drawing of the DH.104 Dove I by E.J. Riding is reproduced with the permission of *Aeromodeller.*

# CIVIL AIRCRAFT IN WHICH ALEX HENSHAW FLEW AS PILOT OR PASSENGER 1946-1948

| TYPE | REG'N | LOCATION & DATE FLOWN |
|---|---|---|
| Miles M.38 Messenger 2C | G-AGUW | Ferry flight from Woodley to Germiston 1946 |
| Short S. 23 Empire Flying Boat | G-AFBJ | Passenger from Durban to Cairo September 1946 |
| Miles M.38 Messenger 4 | G-AHGE | Ferry flight from Cairo to Germiston etc |
| Globe GC-1B Swift | ZS-BKU | Germiston December 20th 1946 |
| Douglas DC-4 Skymaster | ZS-AUB | Passenger from Johannesburg to Heathrow February 1947 |
| Miles M.57 Aerovan 4 | G-AIHJ | Woodley, February 21st 1947 |
| Miles M.60 Marathon (prototype) | G-AGPD | Woodley, February 25th 1947 |
| Miles M.65 Gemini (prototype) | G-AGUS | Woodley, February 21st 1947 |
| Miles M.18 Mk II | G-AHKY | Woodley to RAF Coningsby, March 10th 1947 |
| Miles M.65 Gemini 1A | G-AISD | Ferry flight from Woodley to Germiston, April 1947 |
| Fairchild Argus (Ranger) | ZS-BLF | From Germiston, May 17th 1947 |
| Miles M.65 Gemini 1A | ZS-BRV | Demonstration flights from June 1947 |
| DH.104 Dove 1 | ZS-AVH | Business flights from Germiston from August 1947 |
| Miles M.38 Messenger 2A | ZS-AVY | From Germiston on September 15th 1947 |
| Miles M.65 Gemini 1A | G-AJTI | From Germiston on September 20th 1947 |
| Miles M.65 Gemini 1A | G-AJTJ | From Germiston on September 20th 1947 |
| Miles M.65 Gemini 1A | G-AJTE | From Germiston on September 20th 1947 |
| Beech 35 Bonanza | VP-? | From Germiston on September 29th 1947 |
| Auster J/1 Autocrat | VP-YFL | From Germiston on September 29th 1947 |

| Douglas DC-3 Dakota | ZS-BCJ | Passenger from Germiston to Blackbushe in December 1947 |
|---|---|---|
| Miles M.65 Gemini (Mk. 3 prototype) | G-AKDC? | From Reading on January 4th 1948 |
| Miles M.65 Gemini | OO-CDP | Ferry flight from Woodley to Leopoldville in January 1948 |
| Lockheed Constellation | NC88832 | Passenger from Leopoldville to Johannesburg on January 14th 1948 |
| Douglas DC-3 Dakota | ZS-BCA | Passenger from Germiston to Blackbushe in February 1948 |